THE ROAD TO REASON

Other books by Pat Duffy Hutcheon

A Sociology of Canadian Education (1975)
Leaving the Cave (1996)
Building Character and Culture (1999)

THE ROAD TO REASON

···

*Landmarks in the Evolution of
Humanist Thought*

Pat Duffy Hutcheon

Pat Duffy Hutcheon

Canadian Humanist Publications
Ottawa Canada

Published in 2001 by Canadian Humanist Publications
PO Box 3769 Station C
Ottawa Ontario Canada K1Y 4J8

Canadian Cataloguing in Publication Data

Hutcheon, Pat Duffy, 1926-
    The road to reason : landmarks in the evolution of
humanist thought

Includes bibliographical references and index
ISBN 0-9686014-1-3

    Humanism--History. 1. Title

B105.H8H88 2001   144   C00-901500-0

Cover created by Richard Young
Text designed by Walters & Greene Associates

Printed and bound in Canada by Tri-Graphic

To the memory of my father, Lewis Benedict Duffy,
whose example planted the seeds of my 'built-in doubter' and
encouraged me to communicate with people rather than with spirits;
and to my son Tom who resembles, in so many ways,
the grandfather he never knew.

*Our lives we borrow from each other
And men, like runners, pass along the torch of life*
—Lucretius,
De Rerum Natura

*I shall be telling them with a sigh
Somewhere ages and ages hence;
Two roads diverged in a wood, and I—
I took the one less traveled by,
And that has made all the difference.*
—Robert Frost,
The Road Not Taken

*I seek in vain to find a resting place
I trudge despairingly this endless road,
How many thousand ages must we wait
'til hope springs blooming from the dusty earth?*
—Omar Khayyam
The Rubaiyat

CONTENTS

....

Preface

About Herman Melville's Captain Ahab, a few of the ship's crew—men of reason—understood. They perceived the horror in his stubborn chase of the great whale. They knew why devastation and death must come. Their Captain's logic, like his seamanship, was impeccable; but the premises from which he reasoned, to which that logic was applied, were insane. Nevertheless, the crew followed that quest of blind hatred to their undoing. I invoke *Moby Dick* because the story is so well known, and still so moving. But the lesson is of far broader application than to Nantucket whalers. It bears upon reasoning, knowing, and acting upon knowledge. The pertinence is self-evident; but it is often overlooked or forgotten, even by philosophers. And it has profound implications for religion, including the secular ones.

Even faultless deduction is powerless to yield truth, or to approach it, if the premises are empty, self-contradictory, or preposterous. The obvious implication for religion is that however proficient the theologians, however evocative and moving their language may be, there is no truth-indicativeness in an exegesis *if* the givens are mad. The brilliant and sometimes irritating David Stove, a great but undervalued philosopher of science, had much to say on the philosophical issue. (He had also some unnecessary things to say about 'Darwinism.') Writing on nineteenth-century Idealism (his essay is subtitled "A Victorian Horror Story") and its style of reasoning, Stove observed that:

> ...here the trouble is just the opposite. The premise entails the conclusion all right, but it is so astoundingly false that it defies criticism, at first, by the simple method of taking the reader's breath away. This was a method which the neo-Hegelian idealists

later perfected: reasoning from a sudden and violent solecism. Say or imply, for example, that in English 'value' means the same as 'individuality.' You can be miles down the track of your argument before they get their breath back.

This method is not only physiologically but ethologically sound. Of course it should never be used *first*. You need first to earn the respect of your readers, by some good reasoning... *then* apply the violent solecism. Tell them, for example, that when we say of something that it is a prime number, we mean that it was born out of wedlock. You *cannot* go wrong this way. Decent philosophers will be so disconcerted by this, that they will never do the one thing they should do: simply say, 'that is NOT what "prime number" means!'

But of course such violent solecisms, utterly counter-factual premises, and mere propositional bluster, have been meat and drink far beyond nineteenth-century Idealism. Idealism was merely a last-ditch, but eloquent effort to save Christianity from the natural sciences. Solecisms have been staples in philosophy since it began, long ago, in dimly lit caves with animals rendered on the walls. As to the religions, profane as well as sacred, for most of them the need to justify absurd premises once their initial shock wears off is blissfully absent. The religious point is precisely *not* to justify the incredible. It is rather that no justification of such premises is needed—that to demand justification is seriously deficient faith—or worse. The best possible consequences of which deficiency are mere poverty, obloquy, or threats. The worst is holy war or the *auto-da-fé*.

There is a generally held goal among all those who have been (what we now call) humanists in the past, and who are humanists today. It is to relieve, of absurd premises, shibboleths, and solecisms, our human capacity for reason and creative imagination. And, for such potential for goodness as may have evolved in us. It is to confront reality armed with all possible tools of cognition, to face the facts of life and nature's workings; to use logic for its real purpose—the pursuit of truth, rather than reaching foregone conclusions from whatever premises are necessary. In short, the common goal of what we call humanism has been to encourage inquiry, honest and competent inquiry. It includes the recognition that even skilled inquiry can yield error, and that therefore human knowledge is only very broadly progressive. Thus the fundamental human obligation must be to examine continuously our beliefs as well as our actions, and to apply to the conduct of life the best approximation of truth available at the time.

Nevertheless 'humanism', as to detail, has meant quite different things to different people. It was nascent, although hardly silent, in the ancient Mediterranean world: Epicurus and Lucretius spoke its Greek and Latin versions. There were notable, and noble, expressions of it much earlier in what were to be India and China. It became a literary, then a general artistic movement on the Italian peninsula in the time of Dante and Boccaccio and Pico, a rediscovery and celebration of art, architecture, and thought recovered from the ancient world. It energized scholarship among a somnolent clergy and among the newly affluent nobility. The spread to northern Europe brought incursions into theology, with what were to be profound, sometimes cataclysmic, social consequences. Philosophy and education were transformed.

But the very core of humanism was itself in gradual metamorphosis, catalyzed especially by the scientific revolution of the seventeenth century and the Enlightenment that accompanied and burgeoned from it. The humanist core was in due course entangled with an extension, sometimes a premature and too-enthusiastic extension, of Enlightenment ideals. The instruments of this expansionism were the adamantine probes of empiricist logic, and also, oddly enough, the Romantic yearnings of Rousseau. But by way of humanism it became possible, for the first time in history, for an independent thinker to proclaim safely, in public, the worth and dignity in principle of *every* human being. The astonishing sequelae of that remain, autocatalytic, all around us, at least in much-belabored Western civilization.

It is thus no small matter to lay bare, within so jumbled a spectacle of cultural history, a truly common set of goals. It is an achievement of scholarship and interpretation to trace it, persuasively, back through the millennia. This Pat Duffy Hutcheon has done in text so lucid, so temperate and modest, that it begs to be read. One fails to notice the special quality of the writing until one stumbles upon one of her two short poems, slipped into the text unannounced and unsigned. Her long career as a teacher, among several other careers simultaneous and sequential, is much in evidence in this exposition. Because, moreover, Pat Duffy Hutcheon's essays succeed individually, their collection in a single volume, arranged by historical chronology, succeeds further by means of its emergent properties. The book as a whole follows the Ariadne-thread of the liberation of human understanding.

Like most threads it is itself spun of strands. The strand that contributes most, today, to the strength of the thread is here identified, as it should be, with evolutionary naturalism. A strand of *general* metaphysical naturalism there has been, of course, from the beginning. Without it there could never have been anything like the ideal, at least, of objectivity, or systematic methods of inquiry and independent verification. Humans have long seen, after all, and expected in all the things and events around them, magic or conscious intention—*purpose*, as Ahab saw it in the white whale. They have imagined in all things and events some form of *will*, like the will of the local head-man or prince, but infinitely more powerful, more demanding of elaborate applause and appeasement if evils are to be kept at bay. Any move toward recognition of a general *human* value, rather than that of the prince and his retinue—an indwelling merit of life itself, independent of any imaginary, inhuman *will*—requires two assumptions about the structures and causes of things and events. First, it requires that they are natural and at some level regular; and second, therefore and in consequence, that they are accessible to honest inquiry. There is no point in trying to know what is in principle capricious, unknowable.

Therefore it is proper to begin a chronologic tour of humanist thought as it is done in these chapters: with the Buddha and with Confucius; with, that is to say, the strong first glimmerings of systematic, generalized rationality. It is fitting, and moving, to encounter at roughly halfway along the course the remarkable Harriet Martineau, a gifted and cheated Unitarian child, who reported long after, having triumphed over some of her adversities, that "it was my fixed resolution never to mortgage my brains."

But it is also proper to complete the survey with the efforts of contemporary scientist-scholar-writers (who stand, however, as always, on the shoulders of giants). And so it ends with Edward O. Wilson and Richard Dawkins, among the many now amplifying what Charles Darwin first provided, one hundred and forty years ago, in its *indispensable, two-part* form: a detailed, logical, naturalistic account of biological diversity and the place within it of human beings, *together with* an algorithmic—that is, a spontaneous, unwilled—mechanism for bringing such diversity into existence.

For it is clear that if the fundamental goal of humanism is the liberation of thought from dogma and the prohibitions laid down by power, so as to effect an emancipation of humanity from literal bondage and exploitation as in our past, then rationalization is needed. Specifically, rationalization is needed of human behavior toward planet Earth and toward humanity itself—toward all members of itself. For that, the central product of humanism must be firm knowledge of human origins, of the position of this species among all others, living and vanished, and of realistic prospects for its continuance and improvement on this, our small home in an unimaginably vast cosmos. And yes: *if* good evidence indicates otherwise and points unmistakably toward an origin of the incalculable diversity of life that is *not* spontaneous, *is* willed, then humanistic thought must lead the way to the acceptance and application of *that* evidence. Because it is real evidence and only real evidence that matters.

But, after one hundred and forty years of exponentially growing science, no such evidence has as yet appeared despite the most heroic efforts to acquire it. And, given that Darwinian evolution is today a body of knowledge interwoven as densely and tightly with the rest of science as are atomic and molecular physics, as intimately as is gravity with cosmology and mathematics with engineering, Darwinian evolution is very, very unlikely to be discarded for something radically different. Ditto, and more so, the scientific naturalism upon which it is founded.

In these essays, Pat Duffy Hutcheon has clearly undertaken over time to prepare for intelligent adults what is effectively a course of study, an annotated history, of the core of humanism.

Assembled in this book, the essays are that much and more. I trust that it will be widely read, so that it may exert some of the counter-influence so badly needed in these times of naive relativism and New Age maundering, primitive absolutisms, populist posturing, and a pervasive faux-spirituality. There is now on record plenty of hard, practical experience in the world, as there was not in Homer's time or that of the early sages of the Middle East, or even perhaps in thirteenth-century Europe, of using logic for deductive operations on *sound* premises—about how the world is constituted. There is plenty of recorded and accessible experience of acting rationally upon the results of such mental operations. All that's needed is enough competent, honest teachers, and students prepared in youth, and willing as adults, to learn. Whether those teachers and adults exist, or will come to exist, is quite another question.

Paul R. Gross
University Professor of Life Sciences Emeritus,
University of Virginia; and
Trustee, American Academy for Liberal Education
Boston, August 14, 2000

Acknowledgements

···

The essays comprising this book have been written at various times and for various immediate purposes over the past decade. This makes it rather difficult to recall, much less include, everyone who may have contributed in some way to the creative and research process. Therefore I will begin with a general note of gratitude for all the thoughtful people with whom I have conversed during those years, whose comments may well have sparked some of the ideas expressed in my writings. After all, that is how cultural evolution works! However, another inherent feature of the type of process from which this book evolved, is that, in the end, the author must bear final responsibility for the culminating product—especially for any omissions or errors contained therein.

That said, I would like to take this opportunity to express my gratitude to all those who contributed to the process of selecting me for the "Canadian Humanist of the Year" award which this book is intended to commemorate. My thanks are due, as well, to Wilfrid Laurier University Press of Waterloo, Ontario, for permission to reprint the excerpt on Harriet Martineau from the chapter on her life and work in my 1996 book, *Leaving the Cave: Evolutionary Naturalism in Social Scientific Thought*. Similar permission for various other components on the part of *Free Inquiry, The Humanist, The Journal of Educational Thought* and *Humanist in Canada* is greatly appreciated as well.

With the publication of most books, there is usually one person whose contribution is so central to the success of the enterprise that it is difficult to imagine how it could have come to fruition without him. The key person in this instance is Dr. David

Blackwell, Vice President of Canadian Humanist Publications. Words fail to express the depth of my appreciation for the dedication, humour and expertise with which he performed his critical role of coordinator, expediter and ultimate editor of the entire project.

As in the case of my previous books, no list of acknowledgements would be complete without mention of the consistently wise advice of my husband Sandy, and the dependable support of my family. Among these I would particularly like to note the ever-ready helping hand of granddaughter Jennifer Hutcheon; grandson Shane Westcott who delivered and installed the new computer parts and programs that made the book's speedy finalization possible; and daughter-in-law Dr. Wendy Hutcheon who is perpetually on call as a trouble shooter for my much-maligned and mishandled machine.

I will also be forever grateful to Drs. Blodwen and Joe Piercy, long-time editors of *Humanist in Canada*, for their sustained support and encouragement over the years, and for their scrupulous editing. My appreciation goes as well to the able and dedicated team at Canadian Humanist Publications. This includes Dan Morrison, financial manager, and Dr. Paul Pfalzner, who deserves special mention for his contributions both to the editing process and to our entertaining and creative collective search for a title. I also want to thank my granddaughter Carolyn Hutcheon for contributing the major part of the subtitle. Credit for the final wording of the main title, however, must go to Earl Doherty, who came up with the 'winner'. For the strikingly appropriate book cover I would like to extend my sincere appreciation to the CHP artist and illustrator, Richard Young.

My heartfelt gratitude goes to Theo Meijer, translator, retired educator, member of the Board of Directors of Canadian Humanist Publications and Past President of the B. C. Humanist Association, for his highly professional job of editing. Al Levin, Director of Internet Services, Institute for Humanist Studies and President of the Humanists of Iowa, deserves particular mention for his efforts to provide advance publicity for the current book as well as wide readership for my previous publications; as does Conrad Hadland, leader of the humanist discussion group at the Unitarian Church of Vancouver, who has also contributed significantly in this regard.

I would also like to extend my thanks to those who took the time to read carefully and comment on the various chapters, or to provide me with important sources. This list includes Dr. Barry Beyerstein, Professor of Neuro-psychology at Simon Fraser University, John Moore and Clifton Bennett and, once again, Dr. David Blackwell—whose academic expertise on Albert Schweitzer was most helpful. It also includes Dr. Richard Dawkins, Charles Simonyi Professor for the Understanding of Science, Oxford University; and Dr. Edward O. Wilson, Pellegrino University Research Professor, Honorary Curator in Entomology of the Museum of Comparative Zoology at Harvard and recent winner of the Kistler Prize for his contributions to the introduction of biological thought into the humanities and social sciences.

No list of those who contributed above and beyond the call of duty would be complete without special mention for Dr. Robin Fox, University Professor of Social Theory at Rutgers University, who was kind enough to read the entire manuscript in record time, and whose comments are available for all to see on the back cover. The Omar Khayyam chapter would not speak to me as movingly as it now does without Professor Fox's generous gift of Edward Fitzgerald's translation of the *Rubaiyat*.

Finally, among the most significant of the contributions to the making of this book was that of Dr. Paul R. Gross, University Professor of Life Sciences Emeritus, University of Virginia, and Trustee, American Academy for Liberal Education, who is the author of the Preface.

1: Was the Buddha the First Humanist?[1]

The concepts of Dhamma and Abhidhamma from the Theravada tradition, as taught by the Buddha in the sixth century BCE, are shown to be highly relevant to modern scientific humanist thought.

For the modern humanist one of the most astounding discoveries could well be an early twentieth-century book written by Professor Rhys Davids: a British scholar of the period who specialized in ancient Indian philosophy. Unlike most other works on Buddhism, this one focuses on the Buddhist 'Norm' as actually taught by the Buddha and his students. It deals with what is revealed in the Pali (or Palm-Leaf) Literature of the original Buddhism. These texts, known as the *Three Pitakas* (or Baskets of Tradition) were then in the process of being translated into English for the first time ever, by the Pali Text Society founded by Rhys Davids in 1881. This religious literature is still seldom encountered in the West, where Sanskrit translations of the Maha Yana tradition are much better known. It includes the *Vinaya* and *Sutta Pitakas*—the oldest known records of the Buddha's thought.

Rhys Davids' work differs from that of most scholarly approaches to the subject in that the significance of early Buddhism for scientific humanist thought is recognized throughout. She believed that the Buddha's teachings, as discovered in these records, presented a world view in profound opposition to the Animistic, mystical and absolutist beliefs prevailing throughout human history, not only in Asia but in Western cultures as well. And she was convinced that the key role of the authentic original Buddhism as a forerunner of social science (particularly psychology) had never been adequately appreciated.

Some four decades later, George Santayana summed up the Buddha's accomplishment and the degree to which it marked a courageous, though ultimately doomed, intellectual revolution in the culture of its time and place. "The clearing it made...," he wrote, "was soon overgrown again by the inexorable Indian jungle; but had a virile intellect been on hand [after the Buddha's passing] it would have been free to raise something solid and rational in the space so happily swept clean of all the accumulated rubbish."[2]

Rhys Davids was not so pessimistic about the long-term influence of the original Buddhism—largely because elements of it did, in fact, endure to alter and eventually escape the 'Indian jungle' of the time. Working from numerous clues in the scholarly literature, she was able to judge that the most accurate approximate date of the life of the Buddha, or Prince Gotama Siddhattha (Gautama Siddhartha in Sanskrit) was from 563 to 483 BCE. Given the nature of the then-current Indian culture, and that of subsequent historical eras, she found it unsurprising that Gotama's ideas did not flourish there in the pristine form. "In its motherland," Rhys Davids wrote, "the original Buddhism, in both medieval and modern times, has stood as little chance of being appreciated by Indian philosophers as experimental, evolutionary or pluralistic philosophy is likely to be approved of by students nourished on Thomas Aquinas."[3]

Professor Rhys Davids described how the great religious reform movement that had shaken Northern India during the sixth century BCE moved about a millennium later into Southeast Asia—as the Hina-Yana (Little Vehicle)—and was subsequently able to retain its earlier attributes for several centuries. On the other hand, the parent branch or Maha-Yana (Great Vehicle), while winning in terms of numbers of adherents throughout India, was gradually engulfed and adulterated by the three powerful competing currents in the larger culture. These were the Animism of the common people, the Vedandist beliefs inherited from the Harappa civilization of the third and second millennia BCE; and the caste system established during the later Aryan invasions. Ironically, it was these *departures* from the philosophy of the Buddha that had such powerful appeal for the Chinese, Koreans, Japanese and Tibetans who changed it even more drastically from its original course in adapting it to their own cultures. It is interesting to note that the scholarly group around Professor Rhys Davids appeared well aware that, in this process, Buddhism was merely functioning—much as all great world religions have functioned—as the key vehicle of evolution for the containing culture. Rhys Davids contended that, because of this evolutionary history, the authentic ideas of Buddhism are to be found *only* in the sacred Canons of the *Pitakas* that escaped translation into Vedic or Sanskrit: those of the Hina-Yana (or Theravada) branch confined chiefly to Cambodia, Thailand, Laos, Sri Lanka and Myanmar; and in the scholarly commentary devoted to these. The whole of this is known as the Pali Literature.

The Nature of Reality and Human Consciousness

The author devoted most of her book to a rigorous, scholarly examination of the central ideas of Buddhism, as presented in the ancient *Pitakas* and accompanying commentaries. She began with the concept of Dhamma (a term similar to the 'Dharma' of Vedantist tradition but employed quite differently by early Buddhists) and with the unique concept of Abhidhamma. For Gotama Siddhattha, Dhamma represented the eternal and natural order of things, propelled not by a deity but by necessity. It implied no creation, purpose or ending; no plan traceable to a mysterious consciousness prior to, or transcending, that of humans. Rhys Davids' study of these oldest known books on Buddhism reveals a universe that contains many worlds, without a 'first cause'; going on from everlasting to everlasting, by alternating integration and disintegration. This cosmic process is orderly in its psychological and moral as well as its physical manifestations; that is, cause and effect operates equally in both.

Gotama's concept of Abhidhamma appears to be a supremely naturalistic and psychological one as well. It refers to the representation within the human mind of the external order of things and events. It is the logical system for organizing and interpreting experience constructed by human mental capacities during the process of experiencing external phenomena: the instrument regulating the mind. Some twenty-three centuries were to pass before the idea was taken up and further developed by David Hume, Herbert Spencer, Bertrand Russell and Jean Piaget—among others. For the early Buddhists, the concepts of Dhamma and Abhidhamma provided a conceptual structure of such power an entire system of logic and a subsequent unification of learning was made possible by means of them. Only Western cultural chauvinism has prevented us from recognizing it as an accomplishment at least equal to that of Aristotle, which occurred considerably later.

The current relevance of these early Buddhist assumptions about the nature of reality and of the human being as a knowledge maker strikes the modern scientific humanist with the impact of a sledgehammer. Because of progress in the philosophy of science and in the behavioural sciences since Rhys Davids' time, the significance of what she described is far more startling than even she was equipped to understand. We might well respond in awe and reverence to a genius of the stature that the Buddha appears to have been.

Rhys Davids carefully documented her claim that the Norm (comprising Dhamma and Abhidhamma) is what defines the Buddha's original world view: a frame of reference within which all other Buddhist concepts must be comprehended. She devoted the remainder of her book to an elaboration of the most central of these concepts. They are the theory of No Soul, the law of causation, the Norm as moral law, the Norm as ideal, and the human quest for the Norm as a way of living and, ultimately, of achieving *Nibbana* (or *Nirvana* in Sanskrit).

The Theory of No Soul

The assumptions about the nature of reality and human consciousness contained in the Norm imply that the human mind comprises complex, previously programmed but experientially conditioned structures with no non-natural soul or spiritual substance hovering in the background. Rhys Davids maintained that this is precisely what the Buddha and the scholars of the Pali tradition were saying. She noted that this denial of any entity not governed by nature's laws was extended, logically enough, "to the whole hierarchy of gods and superhuman beings wherewith the Indian heavens, not to say earth, are so liberally populated."[4]

What little we know of world cultures in the seventh to fourth century BCE leads us to conclude that the age, in India as elsewhere, teemed with Animistic, superstitious, metaphysical and mystical dogmas of the soul. Rhys Davids claimed that the Buddha had attempted a religious reform aimed at deposing them all. But he must have realized that only an indirect approach could be effective. The first step would have required that his followers be persuaded that the idea of a supernatural soul was without meaning within a Norm-ruled universe. In all early Buddhist teachings one can clearly see the attempt to communicate the futility of speculating about the soul: whether it be finite or infinite; material or spiritual; happy after death or miserable; self-made or god-made; eternal or ephemeral. For example, the Buddha is quoted as saying, "Since neither soul nor aught belonging to soul can really and truly exist, the view which holds that this I who am 'world', who am 'soul' shall hereafter live permanent, persisting, unchanging, yea abide eternally: is not this utterly and entirely a foolish doctrine?"[5]

A scholar named Buddhaghosa, writing in the fifth century CE, discussed the five Khandras or categories into which the early Buddhists divided the human organism for purposes of analysis. He began with the body, or the material context within which mental processes occur, then listed the four most basic of these processes: feeling, perception, the will and consciousness. He emphasized that the Khandras were intended not only to incorporate all types of human functioning, but *to afford no foothold for the supernatural and the Animistic*. On the basis of these and similar writings which she was the first to translate into English, Rhys Davids suggested that followers of the original Hina-yana Buddhism laid the foundation for a science of the mind some two thousand years before the first stumbling forays in that direction in the West. She responded to the objection that their work was mere description by comparing that necessary initial task with the premature conclusions of the psychology of her own day—ridden as it was with Freudianism and Jungian constructs. "Surely, to start with description is a better basis for the advance of knowledge than to block the path of inference and synthesis by transcendental agencies," she said.[6] She considered the Buddha's understanding of the nature of consciousness to be far more sophisticated than were the prevailing ideas of her own time. She quoted him as follows:

> Consciousness is reckoned only in accordance with the condition causing it; visual cognition from sight and seen object, idea from mind and mental object. Just as fire is different according to its fuel. Do you see that this is a becoming and not a being? Do you see that the becoming is according to a stimulus? Do you see that if the stimulus ceases, that which has become ceases?[7]

The Nature of Causality

There *was* a self-transcending continuity in the Buddha's scheme of things, but it was not a conscious soul. It was the ongoing stream of organic life. Only if this is understood can early Buddhist thought be comprehended on its own terms, according to Rhys Davids. And only on those terms can we appreciate its significance for psychology and for modern humanism. It appears that the Buddha took a bold and remarkable stand against the theories of his day. He taught that all things-as-known are caused by what went before: that all life is a coming-to-be through one state of organic life inducing another state, organism to organism, antecedent to consequent, world everlasting. The Buddha's teachings affirmed, for the first time in human history, a natural organic and psychological order in which humanity could locate itself; and he presented it as a belief system for all, in direct contradiction to the Animism and mysticism of prevailing thought.

It is sometimes claimed that the Pali literature of Theravada Buddhism presents a philosophy of life rather than a religion. However, this is a fruitless argument in that there was no recognition in those times of any such dichotomy in the culture. 'World view' is perhaps a more fitting concept for this ancient naturalistic belief system which Davids credited with nourishing the roots of what we today call 'humanism'.

The idea of natural causation in what we commonly refer to as the physical realm is nothing new to modern thinkers. What makes the Buddha's theory appear prescient to us today is that it was one of monism rather than dualism: it recognized no limits to natural causation. For the Buddha the law of cause and effect applied equally to all aspects of existence: organic and inorganic, to the mental and moral as well as the physical. He used the term Dhamma to symbolize the Norm, or universal causal order. The aspect of this view most at variance with the dominant dualism of the following centuries is the idea that the Norm applies just as compellingly to human mental operations and moral strivings as to the physical realm to which science has typically been restricted. This is a distinctively Buddhist principle—very far from the Vedic creeds of the Aryans and the dualism of either Plato or Descartes, both of which came later. Rhys Davids explained it as a moral creed depending upon neither revelation nor divinely inspired personal intuition, nor upon the admonitions and threats of human authority figures. It taught the truth and necessity of *moral obligation* throughout and beyond the individual life span, for as long and as far afield as the necessary consequences of that individual's actions impinge upon the future.

The Buddha accomplished this revolution in world view by substituting a cosmodicy for a theodicy, a natural order of cause and effect for the moral design of a creative and punishing deity. This order does not involve the common Western notion of a divine plan working through and within nature, wherein justice is supposedly achieved in the form of supernaturally inspired punishment or reward in this world or in a Heaven or Hell beyond human existence. The Buddha's natural order was, instead, based upon a few fundamental principles. The first principle is that certain acts—whether motor, vocal or mental—inevitably bring pain over the long term to all concerned, while certain other acts bring pleasure or happiness to all, providing the time frame and interpersonal context is sufficiently extended. The second principle is that human beings are defined by how they *behave* (as characters in formation rather than as static essences or souls). The third is that human existence involves, not an aggregate of individual lives, but an evolving system of life: a social organism comprising but transcending the life span of the single person.

Rhys Davids quoted a verse summarizing these principles from a fable found in a *Pitaka* book on the moral teachings of early Buddhism. It will sound familiar to most readers.

> *According to the seed that's sown,*
> *So is the fruit ye reap therefrom.*
> *Doer of good will gather good,*
> *Doer of evil, evil reaps.*
> *Sown is the seed, and thou shalt taste*
> *The fruit thereof.*[8]

It is inevitable that the new wine of the Buddha's ideas had to be conveyed in the old bottles of Animistic metaphor. So we sometimes find references, even in the *Pitakas,* to the Vedantist notion of transmigration of the soul, with each succeeding life being determined by current behaviour. But Rhys Davids was convinced that this doctrine is entirely contradictory to the Buddha's theory of No Soul. In fact, she said, his teachings make no consistent sense unless one views life not in terms of the individual, but as an evolving complex of organisms within an ecological system: all subject to cause and effect. Only in a non-anthropocentric and evolutionary frame of reference can we recognize the power and relevance of the Buddhist Norm as a moral (and psychological) law.

Living the Good Life

What of the Norm as an ideal? Its function is to order the contents of experience into a scale of values, and the things of topmost value into ideals which people strive to realize. For the follower of the original Buddha, judgment of values according to the Dhamma is called a Right-view or Dhucca. Recognition of Dhucca must involve, not resignation but revolt and escape from evil or ill. Such avoidance requires that one follow the Right-way, or Threefold

Training. The critical first stage concerns the development of morally healthy habits, or *Sila* (equivalent to Numbers 3, 4 and 5 of the Eightfold Path). Here we have the precepts of Buddhism, involving abstaining from taking life, stealing, lying, gossiping or slandering, and indulging in alcohol or impure sexual practices. The second level, training in *Samadhi* (Numbers 6, 7 and 8 of the Eightfold Path) involves a disciplined culling away of anything that might hinder the achievement of a higher quality of life, such as lust, anger, hatred, illusion and error. The ultimate attainment of *Nibbana* (or *Nirvana*) represents an acceptance of nature's way, the realization of being part of a single stream of life evolving into eternity. It is a rounding off of life's pilgrimage, to be achieved through moderation rather than fanaticism, asceticism or indulgence. And it predicates nothing about any identifiable existence of the perfected self after death. Concerning death, the Buddha is said to have referred simply to a 'going out' wherein there is no residuum of life.

To achieve this culminating condition of moral purity and intellectual Enlightenment, the *Pitakas* prescribe three grades of moral training or *panna* (corresponding roughly to Numbers 1 and 2 of the Eightfold Path). These are the higher ethics, the higher consciousness and the higher wisdom. The first involves the disciplining of everyday conduct; the second, the training of intellect, emotion and will; and the third, the application of this advanced moral outlook and trained mind to the problems of life. Matters to be understood at this stage involve: (1) the nature, causes and abolition of evil and suffering; (2) the impermanent nature of the external world and everything in it; (3) the impermanent nature of the individual person; (4) the non-existence of a permanent, transmigrating soul; (5) the nature of goodness; and (6) the nature of moral and intellectual emancipation.[9]

It is not possible to do justice to the scholarship of Rhys Davids, nor to her subject, in a summary such as this. The intention is merely to render a little more understandable and accessible the magnificent accomplishments of the great man about whom she wrote: Prince Gotama Siddhattha, whose ideas on psychology and ethics have such an eerily modern ring. And one can only echo

Rhys David's belief that an inquiry into the bases of ancient Buddhism provides the best beginning possible for a study of the evolution of modern scientific humanist thought.[10]

NOTES

1 This is a revised version of an article previously published in *Humanist in Canada* (Summer 1997), 20-23.
2 George Santayana, *The Age of Reason* (New York, NY: Charles Scribner's Sons, 1955), 275.
3. Rhys Davids, *Buddhism* (London, UK: The London and Norwich Press, 1914), 243.
4 *Ibid.*, 52.
5 *Ibid.*
6 *Ibid.*, 63.
7 *Ibid.*, 75-6.
8 *Ibid.*, 123.
9 *Ibid.*, 226.
10 See Richard A. Gard (Ed.), *Buddhism* (New York, NY: George Braziller, 1962), for a comparison of different traditions of Buddhism.

2: Confucius as a Pioneering Humanist[1]

....

The original version of Confucianism is shown to have a distinctively humanist and social-scientific perspective.

It is generally recognized that the study of human society existed long before it was named and formalized as social science in the late eighteenth and early nineteenth centuries. We seldom consider, however, that the enterprise might have originated some twenty-six centuries ago, with the work of an ancient Chinese sage. But there are, in fact, good reasons to conclude this. Chinese historians record Confucius as having lived from 551 to 479 BCE. The word Confucius is the Latinized form of the Chinese K'ung Fu-tzu, meaning K'ung the Teacher (or 'Master').[2] It is not really important whether there was indeed only one man, or a number of similarly inspired men, who—through their participation in the development of Confucianism—came to serve as the personification of ethical and intellectual leadership in the Chinese culture. Arthur Waley, the distinguished British scholar of Chinese antiquity, clearly acknowledged a problem concerning historical evidence of a single source of the tradition when he wrote, "I use the term 'Confucius' throughout this book in the conventional sense, simply meaning the particular early Confucianists whose ideas are embodied in the sayings."[3] What is of significance to us, so many centuries later, is the message or the 'torch' these unknown teachers passed along by means of that name to succeeding generations.[4]

According to tradition, Confucius was marginal in the institutional sense, having failed to achieve the political power for which he yearned. If such was indeed the case, it is likely that this very marginality helped him to develop the critical overview of his time and place that inspired not only his own social reform movement, but a number that were to follow. Although the original version of Confucianism was overwhelmed during subsequent centuries by ancestor worship and exaggerated legalism, a look back at its early form and content may well provide us with a glimpse at this historical example of a distinctively humanist and even incipient social-scientific perspective. The most authentic source of early Confucian thought is considered to be the *Analects*—especially those uniquely ancient books translated by Arthur Waley. As Waley noted, they are the books least coloured by folklore and hagiography. These selected sections of the *Analects* were put together long after the Master is recorded as having died, but *before* they were subjected to centuries of re-interpretation. If there exists any relatively reliable source of the core ideas of Confucianism, it surely must be these books.

Recognizing the Role of Culture

To modern eyes, the world view revealed in the words of the Confucius of the *Analects* may seem neither scientific nor particularly humanist. The two major premises of his thought, as recorded therein, were: (1) the unquestionable superiority of the social order of a previous Golden Age of civilization to that of his own time; and (2) the identification of that Golden Age with a system of moral authority defined and guided by a king, ruling by some sort of divine right. But we must consider the cultural era in which the Master's words were presumably heard, repeated and subsequently recorded by his follower, Mencius, whose life spanned the years from 372 to 289 BCE. During the Chou period in which these men lived, there was no effective central state.[5] Chinese society was divided into warring principalities, with violence and social chaos threatening any established order. Corruption in politics and administration was the norm, and the common people believed in spirits and magical portents of all kinds.

It is easy to understand why a thoughtful social critic of the times might have focused on the historical traditions underlying the cultural and moral order, and on the need for an authority source readily legitimized in the peoples' eyes by those traditions. Should we then assume, as many do, that Confucius was a reactionary authoritarian—or at least the world's first proponent of bureaucratic technocracy? On the contrary, these are modern concepts that do not really get to the heart of the Confucian approach and contribution to human culture. What is important is the fact that *history* was recognized—rather than revelation or divination—as a guide to knowledge about current social problems. And that Confucius is understood to have looked to human authority structures, beginning with the family, rather than to the gods as a source of moral guidance in everyday life.

Thus, the real significance of early Confucianism for the evolution of humanism lies in its emphasis on the *sociocultural context*—rather than the supernatural—as the source and shaper of cultural change. Unlike most theories of the following centuries in all cultures, the original Confucianism identified cause and effect in human society. Confucius and his early followers must surely have been the first known thinkers to recognize the role of culture in human development, and to recommend a balanced view of the nature/nurture issue. In fact, Confucius is quoted as having said that "culture is just as important as inborn qualities, and inborn qualities no less important than culture."[6]

Associated with this sociological and distinctively humanist approach was the Confucian concentration on the concrete rather than the abstract; on group-performed ritual as a means of building morality; and on the cultural and social consequences of behaviour in general rather than on any mysterious inner motivations of the person. Above all, Confucius appears to have been concerned about how human society could be made to work. He is honoured for having introduced the concept of the middle way between extremes: the idea that balance and moderation are virtues in social life, and that compromise is almost always necessary for group living. For example, we are told that the Master said: "A gentleman [meaning a moral person or good citizen] can see a question from all sides without bias. The small man is biased and can see a question only from one side."[7]

Waley concluded that "the success of Confucianism, its triumph over 'all the hundred schools' from the Second Century BCE onwards, was due in large measure to the fact that it contrived to endow compromise with an emotional glamour."[8] Certain other socially and culturally essential qualities were defined as desirable as well. For example, much of the folk wisdom of today can be traced to early Confucian sayings. "Do not judge what is said by who said it!"; "Do to others what you would want done to you!"; and "Always practise what you preach!": all were said first by the Confucianists some twenty-five centuries ago.

Concerning the importance of learning, the traditional Confucius was unequivocal. His advice to rulers was to provide conditions in which people could bring forth children without fear. But when asked what should be done for the people after that, he said: "Enrich them...[and then] instruct them."[9] He apparently spoke a great deal about knowledge. "Shall I tell you what knowledge is? When you know a thing, to recognize that you know it, and when you do not know a thing, to recognize that you do not know it."[10] In early Confucian thought, knowledge comes about solely as the result of learning. "I am not one of those who [claim to] have innate knowledge. I am simply one who loves the past and is diligent to investigate it."[11] Confucius is said to have believed that learning would promote desirable change in the individual—recognizing, however, that change of belief is not universally possible nor even desirable. "It is only the very wisest and the very stupidest who cannot change."[12] With those too foolish or lazy or obstinate to learn, Confucius did not believe in fruitless effort. "Not to talk to one who could be talked to, is to waste a man. To talk to those who cannot be talked to is to waste one's words."[13]

Emphasizing the Practical

Confucius is said to have recognized no mysterious moral order apart from what can be known by means of the human learning process; no dualism of intellect and value, nor of mind and spirit. "One who studies widely and with set purpose, who questions earnestly, then thinks for himself about what he has heard—such a one will incidentally achieve Goodness."[14] Without such an approach, emotion reigns, and "he who is at the mercy of his desires cannot be steadfast."[15] Goodness is then impossible, for "love of Goodness without love of learning degenerates into silliness."[16] In attempting to judge the goodness of others, Confucian advice was intensely practical: "Look carefully into his aims, observe the means by which he pursues them, discover what brings him content—and can the man's real worth remain hidden from you?"[17]

A reform movement emerging from within the Confucianism of the fourth century BCE is known as Mohism, after its founder, Mo-tzu. This appears to have arisen as an attempt to cleanse the philosophy of the fatalism, ancestor-worship and undue obsession with ritual that had gradually accrued in the process of its adaptation to the prevailing culture. Interestingly, Mohism was also opposed to the agnosticism of the original movement, considering it an obstacle to the realization of universal love. This meant that Mo-tzu's movement favoured a return to concern with spirits, presumably for their practical, motivational value. For the most part, however, the ideas taught by Mo-tzu and later generations of Confucianists appear remarkably modern. These thinkers seem to have planted the seeds of logical discourse and empirical description, as well as elements of the Utilitarianism and Pragmatism that only began to re-emerge in Europe and America some sixteen centuries later. And Mencius, who taught that all humans are created morally equal and that government requires the tacit consent of the people, appears to have pioneered the ideals of equality and democracy that we tend to associate chiefly with the Ancient Greeks.

Mencius, like Mo-tzu and many of the Confucianists before him, may well have accepted the conventional wisdom of his culture concerning a twofold universe of heavenly spirits and earthly humans. We have no way of knowing, but if these teachers did assume the existence of gods, they were successful in rendering them irrelevant by promoting a practical outlook that ignored them. For example, tradition tells us that when Confucius was asked how one should serve ghosts and spirits, he answered, "until you have learnt to serve men, how can you serve ghosts?" And when asked about the status of the dead, he said, "until you know about the living, how are you to know about the dead?"[18] He seemed to use the term 'Heaven' in two senses: as fate or chance, or as nature. But in neither sense was it viewed as an entity uniquely concerned with humans. "Heaven does not speak," he is said to have noted, "yet the four seasons run their course thereby, the hundred creatures, each after its kind, are born thereby. Heaven does no speaking!"[19]

Heaven does no speaking, but people do. And there are some great teachers whose words survive like seeds in the rocky ground of recorded human thought for many centuries, ready to spring to life when the soil at long last becomes fertile and the climate supportive. The teachings of early Confucianism about the shaping function of the family—and of custom and expectations—now form the very core of modern sociology. They have stood the test of time much better than many of the scholarly opinions that came later. Mencius deserves universal recognition as an early hero of democracy.[20] Mo-tzu's insights about the practical test of morality underlie a salient approach to modern ethics. And the understanding of cause and effect in the social and moral realm revealed by the founders of Confucianism is astounding, in light of the fact that the concept is still foreign to the world views of most of the earth's inhabitants. All this seems ample justification for modern humanists to glance back at the words of these masters— just as an explorer, in carving out the road ahead, may turn to adjust his bearings by the range of hills behind.

NOTES

1 This is a somewhat revised version of an article previously published in *Humanist in Canada* (Autumn 1997), 22-23; 38.
2 Woodbridge Bingham and others, *A History of Asia*, Vol. I. (Boston, MA: Allyn and Bacon, Inc., 1964), 305.
3 Arthur Waley, *The Analects of Confucius*, 6th Ed. (Northampton, UK: John Dicken and Co., Ltd., 1971), 25.
4 For example, see recent scholarship raising similar questions concerning the historicity of Jesus. An excellent contemporary source is Earl Doherty, *The Jesus Puzzle* (Ottawa, ON: Canadian Humanist Publications, 1999).
5 Stewart C. Easton, *The Heritage of the Past* (Toronto, ON: Holt, Rinehart and Winston, 1964), 156-8.

6 Arthur Waley, *The Analects of Confucius*, 165. Bk. XII(8).
7 *Ibid.*, 91. Bk. IV(13).
8 *Ibid.*, 37.
9 *Ibid.*, 173. Bk. XIII (9).
10 *Ibid.*, 91. Bk. VI (17).
11 *Ibid.*, 127. Bk. VII (19).
12 *Ibid.*, 209. Bk. XVII (3).
13 *Ibid.*, 194. Bk. XV (7).
14 *Ibid.*, 225. Bk. XIX (6).
15 *Ibid.*, 91. Bk V (10).
16 *Ibid.*, 211. Bk. XVII (8).
17 *Ibid.*, 90. Bk. IV (10).
18 *Ibid.*, 155. Bk. XI (11).
19 *Ibid.*, 214. Bk. XIX (6).
20 Edwin O. Reischauer and John K. Fairbank, *East Asia: The Great Tradition* (Boston, MA: Houghton Mifflin Co., 1960), 78-81.

3: What Lucretius Wrought[1]

Lucretius preserved for us, in glorious poetry, the thoughts and wisdom of Epicurus, hence the mainstream science and philosophy of Hellenic Greece.

It is not often that a translator has been as renowned as the great thinker whose ideas he immortalized, but that seems to have been the case with Lucretius, a Roman poet of the first century CE. During his short life he devoted his remarkable literary gifts to reformulating and transmitting anew a centuries-old vision. It was a vision of the 'open society' and of the empirical inquiry method necessary for sustaining it—as the only lasting protection against authoritarianism. The man whose philosophy he rescued from near obscurity was Epicurus, a philosopher and teacher who had spelled out a sophisticated naturalistic world view in Greece during the fourth-to-third century BCE. The Epicurean world view had challenged the reigning dualistic orthodoxies as well as the 'mystery cults'—with their inevitable mysticism, asceticism and pessimism—that characterized the period of turbulent change following the death of Alexander the Great. Everywhere, as their old political system crumbled, people were substituting dreams of otherworldly perfection for what they had come to believe was merely a transitory corporeal existence. Lucretius, writing in another 'time of troubles' when the Roman Republic was being threatened from within, clearly found in the works of Epicurus an inspiration and a potential solution to the follies of his own age.

The Hellenistic philosopher actually produced over 300 'rolls' or books, but only his *Letters* and *Principal Doctrines* have survived. We can credit three great writers with keeping Epicurean thought alive in spite of the 'book burnings' of the centuries following his death. Although the lasting influence of Epicureanism is no doubt largely due to the power of Lucretius' poetry, two later authors also played an important role. One was a Greek satirist and prose writer of the second century CE known as Lucian. The second was the Greek biographer Diogenes Laërtius who died at the close of the third century. In fact, other than Lucretius' masterful epic poem, the chief source on the great philosopher's life and work is considered to be the *Life of Epicurus*, put together by Diogenes from subsequently lost records.

Nonetheless, Lucretius remains by far the most celebrated secondary source of Epicurean thought. "I am treading new ground for a poet," he had written. "It is my great purpose to free men's minds from superstition and [to accomplish this] I am adorning obscure thoughts with the beauty of poetry."[2] Most scholars conclude that it is largely due to the success of Lucretius in achieving his goal that the pronouncements of Epicurus "have come down through the centuries without their relevancy diminished or their wisdom impaired."[3]

What was it that so attracted Lucretius to these pronouncements that he chose to devote the entirety of his all-too-brief professional life to ensuring that they would be readily available to posterity? What was it that had caused these ideas (after the great teacher's death in 271 BCE) to be spread by successors and followers throughout the Greek and Persian world as well as to Rome and Africa? What subsequently motivated Diogenes Laërtius (author of *Lives of the Philosophers*) to devote his talents to reviving and consolidating the message even as the mighty Roman Empire was disintegrating? What enabled Epicureanism to survive as an organized movement for a further two centuries, until it was outlawed and driven underground by Christian Rome?

Most of the insights were not new. One can trace a direct line from Thales in the closing days of the seventh century BCE through Democritus in the fifth century to Epicurus almost two hundred years later. Like his famous Hellenic precursors, Epicurus was an atomist. Also, like them—and the Buddha and Confucius as well—he did not actually deny the existence of the gods. That would have been a too-massive conceptual leap for people of his era. He described the function of gods, however, as strictly ethical in that they represented ideals for humans to strive toward. Also like the Buddha and Confucius, Epicurus was, above all, concerned with defining a world view that allowed for a meaningful moral role for humankind.

De Rerum Natura, Lucretius' great poem interpreting and extolling Epicurean thought, comprises six books in all. Each book is ordered into self-contained sections, designed to develop and drive home a major set of ideas. The first book begins with a joyous (and presumably metaphorical) hymn to Venus, and then presents an introduction to atomic theory. The universe is explained as consisting of an infinite number of atoms: small, indivisible, eternal particles, moving in a space infinite in extent, and periodically uniting into compounds. The second book explains Epicurean ethics and the infamous 'atomic swerve'. (This is widely considered to represent the chief weakness of Epicurean thought. In an attempt to rescue a sovereign human will from the determinism of Democritus, he postulated the strange notion of uncaused swerves in streams of atoms.) The third book returns to the more lasting insights of Epicurus. It covers the structure and essentially mortal and material nature of the soul, as well as the reasons why the premise of mind-body dualism is untenable. The fourth book discusses the Epicurean theory of perception and the role of sex in human behaviour. The fifth provides an overview of the origin of the cosmos, of life, and of the development of civilization—all within an evolutionary frame of reference. The sixth book offers a eulogy to Epicurus and to Athenian civilization in general, and ends with a dark story of calamitous happenings and forebodings about the future.

Initially, it is the beauty of Lucretius' poetry that strikes the reader. Gradually, however, the power of the ideas begins to overshadow even the music of the words. All in all, De Rerum Natura demonstrates the two chief accomplishments of Epicurus as a philosopher: (1) his reliance on a combination of reason and sensation for explaining natural phenomena—rather than on abstract rationalizations grounded in mythology; and (2) his repudiation of the teleological view of nature and of dualism. Truth cannot be found in messages from another world, the philosopher maintained, nor in the neo-Platonic, purely deductive 'sciences' of the music, geometry and astronomy of his day, "which, starting from false premises, cannot be true."[4] He was obviously attacking the ideas of Socrates and Plato, and of Aristotle as well, when he wrote that "fools admire and like all things the more which they perceive to be concealed under involved language, and determine things to be true which can prettily tickle the ears and are varnished over with fine-sounding phrases."[5] Epicurus taught, instead, that truth is derived from the relations among phenomena as they are observed in nature.

There is no divine interference in the natural order of things, according to Epicurus. Far from having been created by the gods, he said, this world has endured for an infinite time. ("We can see that nature, free from divine tyranny, can accomplish all by itself."[6]) He insisted that the soul is a corporeal entity that does not survive the death of the body. Following certain of the earlier Greek naturalists, Epicurus even spelled out the crude beginnings of a theory of natural selection in evolution—anticipating the discoveries of Charles Darwin by over two thousand years. For example: "And many races of living things must have died out and been unable to beget and continue their breed. For, in the case of all things, either craft or courage or speed has from the beginning of its existence protected and preserved each particular race."[7]

Epicurus was particularly prescient in his understanding of cultural change. In fact, he was the first known thinker to apply the concept of evolution systematically to human culture. He traced the evolution of language from its roots in the simple gesturing and vocalizing basic to all animal communication. He explained the evolutionary source of religion in similar terms. "And now what cause has spread over great nations the worship of ... the gods?... [People] would see the different seasons of the years come round in regular succession and could not find out what causes this to be done; therefore they would seek a refuge in handing over all things to be guided by their god. And they placed in heaven the abodes and realms of the gods, because night and moon are seen to roll through heaven and because ... [it is the source of rain and thunder and lightning]."[8]

He believed that religion has done great harm to humankind whenever it has tended to exacerbate a fear of death, and then—in a vain attempt to lessen this artificially induced fear—to buttress the incredible and dangerous belief in individual immortality. As Lucretius put it, "Even if time were able to gather up our matter after death and put it once more into the condition it now is, and if the light of life were to be given to us again, this result would not concern us at all, once the chain of self-consciousness has been snapped asunder."[9]

Epicurus' overriding concern was the need to spell out a naturalistic basis for morality, to replace that which was grounded in supernatural directives. He believed that the roots of this could be found in the sensations of pleasure and pain common to all living organisms. The sensation of pain would have been a signal to animals and early humans to avoid whatever had preceded it, he said. The lasting experience of pleasure would have functioned similarly in the opposite direction. (It is easy to recognize in all this the seeds of the 'associationism' and Utilitarianism of Enlightenment times.) A major source of lasting pleasure for humans is *friendship*, Epicurus thought. Indeed, the highest Epicurean ideal was what we would now call a 'platonic' relationship among equals in which the discussion of ideas and the celebration of life's simple pleasures was unhindered by the constraints introduced by sexual preoccupations. Happiness was viewed as the greatest good, but it was an enduring happiness derived from concern with *consequences* for self and others—not measured merely in momentary pleasure. (For Epicurus, this was why reason functioned as an essential aspect of the process.) Pleasure, in turn, was defined as "freedom from pain and care".[10] All this is very different from the hedonism of which Epicurus was subsequently accused by Cicero, who was the source of the vituperative misrepresentation of Epicureanism that prevailed until the onset of the Renaissance era.

It is impossible to appreciate the significance of Epicurean friendship as the ultimate source of happiness (and the corresponding downplaying of sexual relations) without some understanding of the culture in which the great philosopher came to manhood. Homosexuality had been widespread in Greek society for some centuries. By the time of the death of Alexander the Great, the celebrated cultural norm among the citizenry was a pattern of older married man and youthful male lover(s)—with a wife relegated to the role of mere household manager and child-rearer. Epicurus had become convinced that the predominance of homosexual relations in his era was beginning to destroy the value of, and the very possibility for, authentic *friendship* among men.[11] He also believed that it was the chief cause of his culture's downgrading of the female. He seems to have concluded that the best way to promote female equality was to replace the homosexual cultural ideal with that of intellectually based friendship across and within the genders. Consequently, Epicurus welcomed women to his school on an equal footing with men—something that was then so revolutionary that he was universally reviled for it.

This was only one of the many Epicurean teachings that aroused enmity in Roman and early Christian times. A biographer notes that "for a thousand years the Christian church was successful in burying Epicurus in a sepulchre in hell".[12] But not totally. Horace and Virgil had been influenced by him and, wherever their poetry was read, some Epicurean ideas lived on—continuing to survive in small pockets of the Byzantine Empire and, later, in the early Islamic one. It was not until the Renaissance began in Italy, however, that Western Europeans once more had access to Epicurean thought.

One of the first declared Epicureans was Lorenzo Valla, who was papal secretary to Pope Nicholas V in the early fifteenth century. He wrote at some length on the subject, explaining that the charge of hedonism with which the philosophy had been saddled was totally unwarranted.[13] Then, in 1473, Lucretius' now-famous poem was printed in Brescia on one of the new printing presses. Epicurean ideas began to infiltrate the monasteries, and were encountered and greatly admired by Erasmus. The defining work on Epicurus by Diogenes Laërtius was printed in 1523 in

Basel. Later that century, Giordano Bruno was forced to leave the Dominican order for harboring Epicurean beliefs. He was burned at the stake on February 17, 1600. This was the climate in which Michel de Montaigne read Lucretius and dared to express, in his *Essays,* his own version of an Epicurean philosophy that would eventually help to lay the foundations for modern scientific humanism.

NOTES

1 This is a revised form of an article previously published in *Humanist in Canada* (Winter 1997/98), 20-22.

2 Lucretius, *De Rerum Natura*, Ed. and Trans. Cyril Bailey (Oxford, UK: Oxford University Press, 1947), 756.

3 George A. Panichas, *Epicurus* (New York, NY: Twayne Publishers, 1967), iv.

4 *Ibid.*, 101.

5 Lucretius, *De Rerum Natura*, Ed. and Trans. H. A. J. Munro (Cambridge, UK: Deighton Bell and Co., 1886), 15.

6 Cyril Bailey, *De Rerum Natura*, 971.

7 H. A. J. Munro, *De Rerum Natura*, 136.

8 *Ibid.*, 144-5.

9 *Ibid.*, 77.

10 Cyril Bailey, *De Rerum Natura*, 796.

11 George A. Panichas, *Epicurus*, 119.

12 *Ibid.*, 135.

13 Edward M. Burns, *Western Civilizations*, 4th. Ed. (New York, NY: W. W. Norton, 1955), 357.

4: The Epicurean Humanism of Omar Khayyam[1]

An intriguing story of the perilous philosophical route which led from Epicurus in Ancient Greece to the humanism of Renaissance Europe.

The man who was to keep the torch of scientific humanism alight within early Islamic civilization was born a thousand years after the death of Lucretius, and into a vastly different cultural setting. Nevertheless, in all that Omar Khayyam wrote one can clearly recognize the influence of the great Roman poet, and of the naturalistic Epicureanism that he celebrated. This is doubly remarkable when we recall that, during the centuries between Lucretius and Omar, a Dark Age had engulfed and stifled Western Europe. The spread of a mystical form of religion throughout the remnants of the Roman empire, combined with the influence of the Germanic tribes invading from the north, had gradually produced what amounted to a reversion to barbarism. Gullibility and ignorance pervaded life at all levels, while economic activity declined to primitive levels of barter. An attitude of contempt for earthly existence and bodily pleasures had become the norm, along with belief in all manner of superstition and magic.

Southward and eastward, however, two different cultural patterns had emerged. One was the Byzantine Empire—populated by Hellenized Central Asians: Greeks, Syrians, Jews, Armenians, Egyptians and Persians. It existed as a static, class-dominated, authoritarian society, with change occurring only in extreme form and imposed from without. Yet, by the sheer fact of its existence, in those first cruel centuries following the fall of Rome, this remnant of the ancient civilizations performed a critical holding action for human culture. Within it were preserved many of the achievements of the Hellenic and Classical world. Then, in the seventh century, came the emergence of a new religion among the Arabs and Bedouins to the south, sparking a civilization which eventually encompassed and surpassed what little there had been of original Byzantine achievement.

Mohammed, who established the religion of Islam, became at the same time the founder of a new Arabic state with its capital at Medina. In the century following his death the Islamic rulers (called Caliphs or successors to the Prophet) expanded their jurisdiction from the Arabian Peninsula west to Morocco, north to Spain and Armenia and eastward to Persia, Palestine, Syria and even to the borders of India. By the time another century had passed, however, the over-extended Saracenic empire had begun to disintegrate, with Baghdad emerging as the centre of an independently functioning eastern part. In 1055, the Sultan of the Seljuk Turks conquered the city, assuming complete control over what was by then the Oriental Islamic Empire.

Baghdad is crucial to any story of the history of humanism. It was there that the transmission of Classical learning to the West really began. Learned Jews and free-thinking Persians with roots in both the Byzantine and Saracenic cultures were the heroic preservers of Greek, Roman and Oriental knowledge for more than five centuries. The result was that the ancient Classics, translated from the original Greek to Arabic by the Persian and Jewish scholars at the university and other centres of learning in Baghdad, eventually found their way to the Muslims in Spain. When Sicily, under Muslim control for 130 years, fell to the Normans in 1091 it, too, became a thriving source for the spread of Arabian science and medicine into the rest of Europe. From such centres powerful ideas from antiquity were disseminated, typically by Jewish scholars who wandered from monastery to monastery throughout Christian Europe. Thus were the sparks of learning provided for the flickering candles in those lonely outposts, where Christian monks laboured to translate the Greek and Arabic into Latin and, in the process (no doubt unknowingly), to ignite the conflagration of the Italian Renaissance.

The story of Omar Khayyam's role in all this is a fascinating one. He was born in the eleventh century, at Nishapur (or Naishápúr). His birthplace was, at that time, the third or fourth most important city in the world. It was the capital of the prosperous province of Khorasan, or what was then called Khorassán. His family was Persian, and probably affluent, for he was given the best education available. At his university the dominant philosophy seems to have been that sophisticated meld of Platonic and Aristotelian ideas elaborated by the Persian scholar Avicenna during the previous generation. But other influences were present as well. One of his biographers notes: "In that province of Khorasan where Omar was born, followers of the Buddha... had for centuries existed."[2]

Significant also was the presence of the Brothers of Purity, a group of philosophers similar to the French Encyclopedists of a much later era. These scholars "conducted their speculations on a materialistic plane and attacked all problems with the instrument of human understanding. They had a bias to natural science and tried to found a philosophy on its discoveries."[3]

Omar lived from 1048 to 1131. During the decades preceding his birth, Turkish tribes had been steadily encroaching on the settled land from the north. In 1055, Seljuk mercenaries within the empire rebelled and joined the invaders, and all of Persia fell. Seljuk Sultans then established themselves in Baghdad. By the close of the century, as Omar approached middle age, the conquerors had accepted Islam and were enforcing it with all the ferocity and fanaticism of the recently converted. Utterly unskilled in government and administration, they depended—even more than had the Caliphs—on their Persian advisors.

Sometime after graduating, Omar had entered the service of the Seljuk Sultan Malik-shah, with the understanding that he would be free to pursue the unfettered study of science. It appears that this enviable and protected role was obtained for him through the auspices of an old school friend, Nizàm-al-Mulk. The latter had become Vizry to the former and current Sultan, who were the son and grandson respectively of Toghrul Beg the Tartar—founder of the Seljukian Dynasty. It was the excesses of the latter that were to provide the excuse for the Christian Europeans to launch the Crusades.

During his career with the Sultan, Omar wrote ten books. However, only three survived subsequent 'book-burnings': two pioneering treatises on algebra and one book of verse. Along with other leading astronomers, Omar constructed an observatory for the Sultan in 1074. He is also famous for having compiled a set of astronomical tables so complete that they formed the basis for a calendar at least as accurate as the Gregorian one compiled five centuries later. However, before Nizàm-al-Mulk raised him to a position of independence, Omar may have been a tent-maker. Apparently this is what his poetical name (Khayyam) signifies. One of the poems included in Edward Fitzgerald's 1868 translation of the *Rubaiyat* alludes to this, as well as to what befell Omar in later years:

> *Khayyam, who stitched the tents of science,*
> *Has fallen in grief's furnace and been suddenly burned;*
> *The shears of fate have cut the tent ropes of his life,*
> *And the broker of Hope has sold him for nothing!*[4]

The death of the Sultan in 1092 heralded a drastic change in Omar's prospects. His good friend and protector, First Minister Nizàm-al-Mulk, was assassinated soon after, by a fanatical Persian sect of Ismaelis. This double tragedy ushered in a period of religious reaction and dynastic and sectarian conflict, along with international and civil warfare. The Ismaeli sect (ironically, led by another old school friend of Omar) became all-powerful and, in the course of their zealous enforcement of the jihàd, persecution and murder were rampant. As if that were not enough, the First Crusade, pursued by the feudal knights of Western Europe and the feeble Christian court of Byzantium, had begun its incursion into the troubled Islamic empire. In the devastation of Jerusalem that ensued, 70,000 Muslims were murdered, thousands of Jews were burned in their synagogues, and the city's magnificent libraries were destroyed.

We can assume that Omar, who was above all a free thinker, would have felt increasingly imperiled as the new century wore on. A biographer wrote that the last three or four decades of his life were spent "in this welter of fanaticism and superstition, of disorder and brutality."[5] It is easy to imagine how desperate he would have been to express his real thoughts; to pass on something of his philosophy of naturalistic humanism to succeeding generations. The usual methods of the academic were not safe options. In fact, Omar refused to teach—and one can understand why. At least two of his professional contemporaries, not nearly as deviant as he in their world views, had been put to death for heresy.

In such a situation, what remains for the philosopher of integrity but apparently harmless verse? It seems that there is a phenomenon known as 'ketman' which is a Persian proclivity for observing in public the current orthodoxy (no matter how distasteful) while proceeding in private according to one's own lights. It is a way of surviving in dangerously bigoted and authoritarian regimes. Clearly Omar resorted to this, combining it with his own unique survival mechanism in the form of the Persian quatrain: a poetic invention of considerable antiquity.

For at least a century, scholars from both East and West have been studying what has come down to us as the *Rubaiyat* of Omar Khayyam. Much time and many keen minds have been devoted to separating the wheat of his original expression from the chaff of folk accretions, fraudulent imitation, well-intentioned but misleading interpretation and deliberate distortion with malicious intent. The prefaces to Edward Fitzgerald's 1859 and 1868 English translations reveal the then-prevailing disagreement over whether Omar was an Epicurean wastrel intent on over-indulging in wine, women and song, or a mystical Sufi. Happily, modern Persian scholarship is now shedding new light on the issue. Kasra Parichehr claims that the writer of one of the very earliest works in which Omar's quatrains appear identified him as "a philosopher, materialist and naturalist, a 'lost wanderer'."[6] He adds that the subsequently prevalent hedonistic interpretation of Omar's writings is possible only if the more profound aspects of his themes are not recognized.

Another Persian scholar, Ali Dashti, produced the most credible selection of authentic quatrains to date, based on a thorough study of contemporary accounts documenting Omar's abilities, character, philosophical premises and writing style. Dashti was able to make the considered judgment that "at least thirty or forty of these quatrains, scattered in so many sources, are completely consistent in both style and thought, and seem clearly to be the product of a single genius."[7] From these early sources, Dashti formed a relatively clear picture of Omar's beliefs. He took careful note of comments such as "although the learned Omar, Proof of the Truth, did not believe in prognostication by the stars..."[8] On the basis of a great deal of similar evidence he has strongly repudiated popular descriptions of Omar as a sensually indulgent hedonist, or as a mystic. He demonstrated convincingly that the verses emphasizing these orientations were later additions.

It is true that, for a time after Omar's death, the mystical Islamic sect known as the Sufis claimed him as one of their own. However, Dashti concludes that this idea has been thoroughly discredited by modern Persian scholarship. The Sufi-like quatrains were probably added to the repertoire by Sufis who were attracted by the original verses but failed to understand what they were really saying. Indeed, they were warned of their error by a more discerning (albeit disapproving) reader of the period. "In recent times the Sufis have fallen victim to the outward charms of his poetry. They do not realize that these poems are like beautiful snakes, outwardly attractive but inwardly poisonous and deadly to the Holy Law."[9]

The 'true believer' who penned these words was, of course, quite right. He knew his Omar Khayyam. For, as Dashti pointed out, "We can judge from the early authentic quatrains that his thinking on life and death, on the pre-existence or createdness of the earth, on the first cause of creation, and on the possibility of return to one's original form, was very different from that of the theologians."[10]

It was not only that Omar's ideas were in direct conflict with those of every Islamic sect of the period; he also differed radically from the *philosophical* orthodoxy of his age, as expressed in the works of his early intellectual hero Avicenna. In general, the various biographers of Omar Khayyam seem somewhat puzzled by this, for it is apparent that they accept the Platonic-Aristotelian philosophical stance of Avicenna (refined later by Averroes of Cordoba and ultimately inherited by Aquinas) as the most enlightened of the idea systems of ancient Greece.

However, there was another current of thought that would have been translated by the Persians and made available to scholars such as Omar. We know it was present in the Arabic intellectual culture because it was passed on in succeeding centuries through the Moors and Jews in Spain to an awakening Italy. It was the philosophical naturalism of Epicurus: a perspective far more subversive of the status quo than Plato's elitist dualism and Aristotle's reconciliation of reason and faith could ever be. And it comes through loud and clear in the poetry of Omar Khayyam.

Recent research by Persian scholars has unearthed a comment by Omar that reveals something of his uneasy relationship with his fellow scholars.

> We are the victims of an age when men of science are discredited, and only a few remain who are capable of engaging in scientific research. Our philosophers spend all their time in mixing true with false and are interested in nothing but outward show; such little learning as they have they extend on material ends. When they see a man sincere and unremitting in his search for the truth, one who will have nothing to do with falsehood and pretence, they mock and despise him.[11]

We can gather from this that Omar saw himself as above all a scientist, committed (in the manner of Epicurus) to open, critical inquiry into the nature of things. It is not difficult to extract this commitment from those quatrains recognized as definitive by Dashti. One can imagine Omar's frustration at the contradiction inherent in any attempt to pursue unfettered scientific inquiry into all aspects of existence, in an orthodox and authoritarian society intent on setting rigid limits to belief. He must have been fully aware that transgression of those limits meant death. He could have seen only one way to express the tragedy he felt.

> *I cannot hide the sun with muddy clay,*
> *Nor can I probe the mysteries of Fate*
> *From contemplation reason only brings*
> *A pearl that fear will never let me pierce.[12]*

Emerging in many of his quatrains is an Epicurean skepticism concerning the survival of the soul, or of the possibility of the type of human spiritual transcendence taught by the dualistic and mystical philosophers around him. His frequent references to an omnipotent God seem to be solely for the purpose of challenging the concept. Another consistent message in those quatrains now accepted as authentic is that of skepticism concerning final truths or unchallengeable notions about the meaning of life. One can only imagine how dangerous it would have been to express such ideas directly, in that place and time. Yet, through the medium of poetry, Omar could drop hints. An emphasis on the need to seek knowledge of humanity as well as of other aspects of nature is omnipresent. In all the quatrains we find a pervasive concern for a kind of practical, common-sense morality, with a noticeable absence of justification in terms of supernatural or worldly authority.

In addition to the accusation of Sufi-like mysticism, Omar has frequently been charged with pandering to sexual licence, gluttony and drunkenness. It is true that many of the quatrains attributed to him in earlier times seemed to extol excess. However, it has been ascertained by modern Persian scholarship that these were later accretions, written either by his detractors or by supporters who understood neither his use of imagery nor his Epicurean philosophy. For Omar—as for Epicurus before him—wine and female beauty symbolized enjoyment of life in the here and now, rather than in some imagined heavenly paradise. He employed them as metaphors for that fellowship among human beings seen by Epicurus as both a means and tentative end of human existence. Similarly, the clay wine pot so often found in Omar's poetry represents the inorganic matter out of which humanity was formed. It is through the quatrains replete with such references that Omar is revealed as thoroughly Epicurean.

The more one thinks about the overriding naturalism of Omar's quatrains, and the cultural context in which they were expressed, the more remarkable it seems that they were written at all. And once written—that they ever survived. For what followed was worse than even Omar, at his most pessimistic, could have envisioned. Less than a century after his death, the Mongol hordes from the Asian Steppes had reached Naishápúr, devastating the surrounding land and laying waste to the beautiful city and its centres of learning.[13] There is no way to guess the full extent of the destruction of precious manuscripts that occurred during the several generations before the Mongols were converted from their primitive Shamanism to Islam. A student of the legacy of Islam wrote that, after the Mongol invasions, the Moslem world "lost forever its ideal and even its cultural unity."[14] Another concluded that the Mongols "stamped out the fire of learning in the East so effectively that it never recovered."[15]

The immediate result was that the centre of enlightenment moved north-westward in the twelfth century. Four centuries earlier, Islamic Arabs and Berbers from North Africa had invaded and settled in Spain. It was from this community—known as Moors—that wandering Jewish scholars distributed their precious legacy of Classical and Arabian-Persian thought among the far-flung monasteries of Western Europe. Most of those flickers of learning were nourished by Platonic and Aristotelian ideas, and it is chiefly to the refinement of that current of thought by Arabian scholars that we owe the survival of the physical sciences. Nevertheless, there must have been a few Epicurean sparks from material such as Omar's subversive quatrains that smouldered through the centuries until fresh breezes stirred within the process of cultural evolution. Omar could have been thinking about his own version of immortality when he mused:

> *The Moving Finger writes; and, having writ,*
> *Moves on; nor all thy Piety nor Wit*
> *Shall lure it back to cancel half a Line*
> *Nor all thy Tears wash out a Word of it.*[16]

NOTES

1 This is a somewhat revised version of an article previously published in *Humanist in Canada* (Spring 1998), 22-25.

2 Otto Rothfield, *Umar Khayyam and His Age* (Bombay, India: D. B. Taraporevala and Sons, 1922), 20.

3 *Ibid.*, 36.

4 Edward Fitzgerald, *The Rubaiyat, 1859 and 1868 English Translations* (Calcutta, India: Susan Gupta Publishers, 1943), xi.

5 Otto Rothfield, *Umar Khayyam and His Age*, 44.
6 Parichehr Kasra, *The Rubaiyat of Umar Khayyam* (Delmar, NY: Scholars' Facsimiles and Reprints, 1975), lix.
7 Ali Dashti, *In Search of Omar Khayyam*, Trans. L. P. Elwell-Sutton (London, UK: George Allen and Unwin, Ltd., 1971), 38.
8 *Ibid.*, 45.
9 *Ibid.*, 43.
10 *Ibid.*, 66.
11 *Ibid.*, 78.
12 *Ibid.*, 56.
13 For a description of the razing of the Persian cities by the Mongols see Harold Lamb, *Genghis Khan: The Emperor of All Men* (Garden City, NY: Garden City Publishing Co., 1927), 155-161.
14 Ali Dashti, *In Search of Omar Khayyam*, 241
15 *Ibid.*
16 Edward Fitzgerald, *The Rubaiyat*, 1859 Edition, 20.

5: Renaissance Humanism and Its Unitarian Offshoot[1]

How the naturalism of the ancient Greeks surged up again in Renaissance times, then evolved further into both the Humanism and Unitarianism of today.

Most of us are aware that modern scientific humanism is based on the premise of *naturalism* as contrasted to the dualistic *supernaturalism* of traditional world views. We are aware, as well, that the naturalistic world view explains nature as continuous and all-encompassing. Human beings are understood to be integral parts of that nature, with no mysterious access to supernatural forces capable of directing them or rescuing them from their follies. We are also familiar with the idea that naturalism is somehow connected to the great fourteenth-century revival of learning known as the Renaissance. However, not everyone is clear on the relationship between the naturalism that surged up in Renaissance times and modern philosophical humanism. And even fewer of us associate the Unitarianism of today with any of this. But there is a connection among these currents of thought. It concerns their common source.

Ancient Origins of Naturalistic Humanism

The naturalistic world view existed for a very long time before the Renaissance in Western Europe. It had survived as a minor stream throughout history, from at least as far back as the Buddha and Confucius and the Hellenic Greeks of the seventh to fifth century BCE. It was integrated and consolidated for posterity by Epicurus in the Hellenistic era and by Lucretius in Roman times; and was preserved and subsequently transmitted to Western Europe by free thinkers in the Byzantine and Islamic empires. The story of how this ancient evolutionary naturalism eventually came to provide the philosophical roots of both modern scientific humanism and the 'natural religion' of a major defining current within Unitarianism is a fascinating one.

In the first place, one might wonder how the 'naturalism' of the ancients came to be called the 'humanism' of modern times. The answer is that the concept of humanism has itself evolved. Originally, it was the term applied to the perspective of all the Renaissance scholars who worked at translating the writings of ancient Greek and Roman civilization, and thus making them universally available. Opposing this project were the 'scholastics' who suspected (quite rightly) that it would undermine the Christianity for which they were the official apologists.

The Renaissance had begun only very gradually, over many centuries, as the Moors disseminated works from Ancient Greece and Rome and the Middle East through Spain and Sicily, and as European travellers smuggled them out of the Arab world and into the monasteries throughout Italy and beyond. The final impetus, however, was the invasion of Constantinople by the Turks in the mid-fourteenth century. This resulted in a flood of immigrants from the Byzantine Empire to Italy, their baggage loaded with precious manuscripts until then unknown in a Europe which had emerged from its Dark Age only a few centuries before.

Because the bulk of the earliest translated writings were of an artistic and literary nature, the term 'humanist' very soon became associated with the study and celebration of literature and the fine arts—and subsequently philosophy and history were added to the original canon. This new formal learning came to be referred to as the *humanities*. By the late-seventeenth century the humanist label was being reserved for those who taught the humanities. It is a usage that continues within the university community to this day, and it is one of the chief sources of the confusion surrounding the concept of humanism.

Another source of confusion is the fact that the term is

often used interchangeably with *humanitarianism*. The modern humanitarian outlook emerged from the new ideals for humankind that came to the fore in the Renaissance era: ideals that reached their full flowering during the eighteenth-century Enlightenment. One of the new humanitarian ideals was *individualism* (as opposed to the collectivism of the Middle Ages). A second was a concern for the betterment of *this world* (as opposed to the other-worldliness of the Church-dominated surrounding culture). A third humanitarian ideal was an emphasis on *democracy and equality and justice for all* (as opposed to the authoritarianism and elitism of the times).

However, the particular version of humanism that we are tracing here concerns neither the teaching of the humanities nor humanitarianism *per se*. In fact, it did not originally have the term 'human' in it at all. It was a total world view based on the idea of evolutionary change within a natural universe: a process open to study by means of scientific inquiry.[2] Only in North America during the latter part of the nineteenth century did this naturalistic world view become known officially as humanism, although the term remained closely associated with 'the humanities' within the academic community.

The traditional association between naturalism and humanism stems from the fact that much of what was translated from the original Greek into the scholarly Latin of Renaissance times had turned out to be *scientific* rather than literary and aesthetic. It had to do with the ideas of the Hellenic Atomists and Sophists and the Epicureans and Stoics. All of these had attempted to forge a world view that made sense in terms of the science of their time: a science in many ways far ahead of the purely deduction-based variety which had been re-invented by the scholastics during the late Middle Ages. Those Renaissance humanists who were most captivated by the ancient science—and the assumptions about the nature of the universe underlying it—tended to be the more revolutionary thinkers of the period.

Some of the greatest humanists of the age dealt with *both* the literary and the scientific. Copernicus of Poland was one of these. He began by translating a book of Greek verse, but rapidly moved on to astronomy. In the process he discovered some intriguing differences between the thought of the Hellenic Greeks and that of his own period. Their religions had resembled the views of the Buddha and Confucius much more than those of later times, in that they did not put forward a perspective irreconcilable with the common sense and reason and respect for empirical evidence that made science possible. If gods exist, these philosophers said, they too must operate according to the laws of nature. Consequently, religious persecutions of skeptical inquirers such as those common to Medieval times were virtually unknown in the Classical Greek era.

Copernicus, courageously following his ancient forebears, reached the heretical conclusion that "things do not happen as if at the bidding of capricious spirits ..." And that "the discovery of this essential orderliness in nature marked the beginning of what we call science."[3] Copernicus recognized that it was in the sky that the order of nature was first revealed to the Ancients. He decided to go back and begin where they had left off. His discoveries eventually led to the successful undermining of the Ptolemaic earth-centred theory that had prevailed for over fourteen centuries.

Copernicus remained free from persecution during his lifetime. No doubt this was because he was a respected priest and the man who was both mentor and uncle to him was an influential bishop. Another reason may have been that he was working in Poland, one of the most tolerant cultural settings in Europe in that era. Even so, his revolutionary treatise *On The Revolutions of the Heavenly Spheres* was published only as he lay dying in 1543; and his publisher felt called upon to insert a preface which attempted to obscure the major message of the book so as to make it less likely to arouse the wrath of the Church. That wrath did, however, come down in 1600 in all its fury upon the Epicurean and follower of Copernicus, Giordano Bruno, and—several decades later—on Galileo, who had refined and confirmed the Copernican theory.

Historical Roots of Unitarianism

Before Copernicus there had been Lorenzo Valla—secretary to Pope Nicholas V in Italy, and the first Epicurean of the modern era. He used the then-new methods of historical criticism to demonstrate that the 'Donation of Constantine' was a fraud. It was on this document that papal supremacy in the Holy Roman Empire had allegedly rested. This is important to our story for, in doing this, Valla actually planted some of the original seeds of Unitarianism. He was followed by Erasmus who, by expanding on Valla's research, did the same thing for the doctrine of the Trinity. All three men were humanists in the modern philosophical sense, in that they made revolutionary contributions to the revival of the *naturalism* of Hellenic Greece: the way of thinking that had originally given birth to Western science.

Erasmus, known as the father of the Northern Renaissance, was greatly influenced by the writings of Lorenzo Valla. Like Valla, he was educated as a priest and lived during the early sixteenth century—as had that other scientifically oriented priest, Copernicus. Erasmus also resembled Copernicus in the way that he managed to maneuver carefully in a Europe by then growing dangerous for the Epicurean type of humanist. Many later scholars have viewed Erasmus as representing the epitome of Renaissance thought—the man who led European civilization from childhood into adolescence. The Renaissance itself is often compared to that critical stage in individual development when "consciousness of self is sufficiently developed to allow the person in question to stand outside himself and consider his own character and history against the background of Not-Self... It was the revelation of a more mature civilization, and the comparison of Medieval Europe with it, that shocked the man of the fifteenth and sixteenth centuries into self-consciousness."[4] Erasmus' translation of the bible from the original Greek inspired that early hero of today's Unitarians, Sebastian Castellio, to write his courageous defence of another man who was to become a hero of the Unitarian movement. That man was Michael Servetus, who was burned at the stake for his beliefs in 1553.

Servetus had been sufficiently courageous (or foolhardy) to speak and write openly in favour of Arianism, the subversive seeds of which had been planted as early as the fourth century CE. A Christian named A. D. Arius had then initiated what was to become known as the Arian Controversy by claiming that Jesus was more human than God-like. In 325, the outlawing of this 'heresy' by the Council of Nicaea resulted in the official Nicene Creed affirming that God was indeed a Trinity of Father, Son and Holy Ghost. Arianism was then forced underground, re-emerging into the public arena when Michael Servetus began preaching the same message.

Some time after the publication of Castellio's book, at the height of the Protestant Reformation, a group of Italian humanists seeking freedom from all imposed religion carried the Arian ideas of Servetus and Castellio to Switzerland. From there they escaped to a Poland already rendered relatively open to naturalistic thought by the followers of Copernicus. There the anti-Trinitarian movement evolved still further, influenced by another branch which began to flourish in the 1560s as the official religion of neighbouring Transylvania. It is here that we find the name 'Unitarianism' used for the first time. Under the leadership of the Italian humanist, Faustus Socinus, the Polish version of anti-Trinitarianism was established as 'Socinianism' in 1579. Two centuries later it was pioneered in England by Theophilus Lindsey under the name of Unitarianism.

Fortunately for the new movement, Joseph Priestley almost immediately joined Lindsey as its co-founder. Priestley was a leading scientist, and typical of the kind of people who were attracted to Unitarianism. What made it unique among religions at that time was that it provided a world view compatible with science—and capable of evolving along with scientific knowledge—rather than being in conflict with it. Among its members were the most scientifically oriented thinkers of Britain, leading thinkers who had accepted the essential premises of naturalism along with those of Enlightenment humanitarianism. They believed that religion must give way to science as the source of knowledge about reality and focus, instead, on ethics; and they were looking for a belief system that could accommodate these premises. *Natural religion* was the watchword in the eighteenth and nineteenth centuries.

One might ask, why religion? Why not merely a philosophy? The fact is that the two were virtually synonymous in those times. All world views were defined as ultimately religious in nature. And people wanted the ethical guidance and the framework of ritual for celebrating life's passages and triumphs that traditional religion had provided. In other words, they did not want to throw out the baby of organized service to essential human needs with the bathwater of supernaturalism.

One of the forerunners of the new movement in England was Isaac Newton. Historians usually refer to him as Unitarian even though the denomination had yet to be established in England when he was alive. He was representative of the British Unitarians of the following century in that he spelled out a position of deism acceptable to people who were ready to discard beliefs in supernatural guidance but could not quite bring themselves to part with the notion of a Creator or First Cause of some kind. Nonetheless, they wanted their Creator in some relatively harmless, non-interfering, non-personal form that would not pose a threat to scientific progress.

The deism which Newton had helped to popularize among Enlightenment thinkers such as Locke and Voltaire was ideal for this purpose. One might even argue that it was an essential first step toward the fully fledged naturalism that was to come later. All of the early pioneers of naturalistic humanism, such as Thomas Paine, were deists. Deism allowed for the possibility of a First Cause and preliminary Design, while emphasizing a non arbitrary, all-encompassing natural order flowing from this: an order operating according to laws of cause and effect as manifested in regularities experienced by humans. Understandably then, the new deism gave a great impetus both to science and to Unitarianism—the first religion rooted explicitly in the findings of science. (This notion of the Creative Designer was to persist among scientists until it was rendered untenable by the revolutionary scientific breakthrough of yet another Unitarian, Charles Darwin, and was generally replaced as the foundation of naturalistic humanism by the non-theistic, scientific agnosticism of Thomas Huxley. To this day, however, almost half of the practising scientists in North America can be classified as 'theistic evolutionists', the modern form of deism.)

Priestley established a new Unitarian church in Birmingham

in 1780. As its guiding philosophy, he spelled out a version of deism which he called Necessarianism. One of the first members of his congregation was Erasmus Darwin, grandfather of Charles and an early evolutionist. Like Darwin and other new members, Priestley was heir to the naturalistic current in both Renaissance Humanism and the eighteenth-century Enlightenment flowing from it.

Unitarianism in North America

We cannot leave Priestley's story, however, without tracing the course of his influence, and that of Unitarianism, into North America. His Birmingham ministry had ended precipitously on Bastille Day in 1791. He and his family, all set to celebrate both the American and French revolutions, were attacked by a mob and their home destroyed by fire. It was not only Priestley's political allegiances that had infuriated the populace; the new scientifically based Unitarian religion was especially inflammatory. This is how it happened that one of Britain's greatest scientists—the discoverer of oxygen and a prestigious member of the Royal Society—was virtually run out of his own country. He was forced to move first to London (where he was ostracized even by fellow members of the Royal Society) and then, with the encouragement of Thomas Jefferson, to the United States. Priestley settled in Philadelphia where, in 1796, he established a Unitarian society based on his ideas. Actually, it was the third such congregation in America by then. By then, as well, famous Americans such as Benjamin Franklin and Thomas Jefferson, who had known of Priestley's ideas for some time, were considering themselves Unitarian.

There is a great deal more to the story of the evolutionary naturalism forming the foundations of both philosophical humanism and Unitarianism. If space permitted we could trace the various waves of reaction to naturalism that have periodically swept over Priestley's 'natural' religion. Much of this was the result of the entrance of new tributaries carrying more traditional religious ideas back into the mainstream of Unitarianism. This happened rather quickly in both England and Ireland, as a liberal form of Christianity soon began to make inroads into the movement. In

New England, one such early tributary was the Arminianism introduced to Europe in the early days of the Reformation by Jacobus Arminius of Holland. For the descendants of the Puritans who brought it to the New World, Arminianism had come to represent the liberal arm of Congregationalism. The latter was the name chosen to reflect their non-centralized denomination as it had evolved in the pioneering colonies.

The New England Arminians, following in the footsteps of the founder of their philosophy, were mainly rationalistic dualists rather than naturalists. However, they melded well with the Unitarians of the Priestley tradition who were embracing the discoveries of Isaac Newton in physics and the work of John Locke in psychology. The Arminians promoted a rationalistic view of the world which incorporated both Gottfried Lessing's idea of an ongoing form of revelation and the 'Argument from Design'. This philosophy became so popular with the American intellectual elite that, in 1805, Harvard University elected an Arminian president, Henry Ware. Twenty years later, when the Arminians of New England joined the Unitarians to form the American Unitarian Association, Harvard was recognized as a Unitarian institution.[5]

Another tributary flowing into early nineteenth-century Unitarianism was Emerson's Transcendentalism. This posed far more of a threat to the naturalistic base of the religion than had Arminianism because, with its reliance on a mystical form of personal intuition as the ultimate arbiter of truth, Transcendentalism virtually opened the door to Aristophanes' 'cloud cuckoo land'. William Henry Channing, a leading Unitarian minister of the time, was particularly concerned about the potential for subjective relativism that he recognized in the popular new philosophy. Like all cultural trends celebrating egocentrism, however, Transcendentalism proved to be highly infectious. In Britain from the mid-nineteenth century on, it became evident that James Martineau (a leading Unitarian theologian) was beginning to steer the denomination there toward a related version of transcendental Christianity. Ironically, near the end of that century, the Reverend Martineau was one of the most vocal critics of both Priestley's Necessarianism and Darwin's new theory of evolution.

Unitarians Revisit Their Humanist Beginnings

The story turned out to be quite different in the American Midwest and Western states—and throughout Canada, except for a small enclave in the East that was influenced by the more Christian ministries of Ireland (the homeland of the country's first Unitarian minister) and New England. In fact, from the 1860s on, what was by then known as humanism was well on the way to becoming the prevailing world view of North American Unitarian congregations and their ministers. And even in New England, the more practical, social-action oriented stance of Theodore Parker was replacing those of both the earlier Arminianism and Emerson's Transcendentalism in Unitarian pulpits. Parker taught that "what was eternal was the moral element in religion."[6] And as for miracles, he had "only pity for those who sought in the aberrations of nature some divine revelation."[7]

By the turn of the century, however, it was the ideas of John Dewey, the great American philosopher of naturalism, that lived in the sermons of the ministers and in the religious education programs of the Unitarian church schools. As one historian put it: "Humanism swept through the denomination... Advocating science against supernaturalism, democracy against tyranny, reason against superstition, experience against revelation, humanists plowed new ground among Unitarians..."[8] In fact, the Humanist Manifesto of 1933 was prepared and signed chiefly by Unitarian ministers. Another often neglected fact is that Unitarianism (along with the Ethical Culture movement) was largely responsible for nourishing the philosophy of naturalism in North America for the better part of a century.

What we now consider 'evolutionary naturalism' is the philosophy underlying and defining the modern humanist world view. It is not the same thing as the celebration or worship of humanity, and of our artistic and literary creations. Nor does it imply an idolizing of science and technology, although mystics and supernaturalists often accuse humanists of that. Nor is a commitment to humanitarianism sufficient to define one as a philosophical humanist—for most of the world's religions share that commitment, in theory at least. And, although academics continue to reserve the label of humanist for scholars in the humanities, that usage totally ignores the *philosophical premises* of the scholars in question, and of the original movement. To repeat, the defining feature of modern humanism—what distinguishes it from other world views—is its underlying philosophy of evolutionary naturalism.

This naturalistic brand of humanism is also the world view which constituted the very core and reason for being of Unitarianism from its birth and through much of its history. It was what made it distinctive as the only natural religion of modern times. It provided Unitarians with the ultimate premises of their unique world view—unique among modern religions, that is. It was this naturalistic world view—rather than the mere non-orthodoxy and belief in the cult of the individual so popular in Unitarian-Universalist circles today—that marked early Unitarianism as different from other religions.

There is indeed a clear distinction between the world view of modern naturalistic humanism and all those variations on supernaturalism that form the basis of most religions and philosophies. This stems from the fact that modern humanists (following in the steps of the pioneers of Unitarianism) believe all existence to be within, and of, and *confined to* evolutionary processes within nature.

Certain key premises concerning the nature and source of the 'good' follow from this. Humanist Unitarians believe that humans can only recognize good values and principles for living by experiencing (either directly or vicariously) the consequences of having lived in terms of them. This is not as difficult as it seems, for we have the entire historical record of the human race to base our judgments upon. We can take note of what happened over the long term, and for all those concerned, when people behaved in certain ways. Humans can assess the wisdom and effectiveness of traditional rules of conduct, and not be too inclined to jettison them recklessly because times have changed. We can employ common-sense reasoning, combined with the most reliable of our findings in the life sciences and social studies, to predict that some actions are harmful to self and others and some are helpful over the long run; that some are likely to be destructive of life and of individual fulfilment, while others are more apt to bring about constructive ends for the individual and the social group and the ecology. We can seek universal values transcending place and time and culture and religious doctrine: values that are grounded in our common evolutionary origins and biological needs and propensities; in our shared human need to live in groups; and in our joint responsibility for the survival of life on this planet.

The same applies to the premises held by humanist Unitarians about the nature of knowledge. Like all philosophical naturalists they are committed to the evidence of communicable, joint, publicly testable observation—combined with our precious human reason as the means of making connections among experienced regularities. Humanists believe these sensing and reasoning tools are the *sole* means available to fallible humanity for building and confirming reliable knowledge claims. Other sources of so-called 'truth' are recognized as no more than seductive delusions. Examples of such delusions are belief in the infallibility of revelation and personal intuition—or in messages from the so-called universal Consciousness now being touted by the pseudo-scientific mystics among us. According to members of the Unitarian humanist community, all these imagined sources of truth have been shown throughout history to be unreliable and often highly dangerous. They remind us that no one ever condemned people to death in the name of reasoned skepticism and the rules of scientific inquiry, but rivers of blood have flowed in the service of unchallengeable supernatural revelations and personal intuitions. It was those all-too-costly certainties that the first Unitarians rejected when they based their great experiment in 'natural religion' upon the methods and findings of the science of the time.[9]

NOTES

1 This is a slightly revised version of an article previously published in *Humanist in Canada* (Summer 1998), 22-27.
2 See Pat Duffy Hutcheon, *Leaving the Cave: Evolutionary Naturalism in Social Scientific Thought* (Waterloo, ON: Wilfrid Laurier University Press, 1996) for an explanation of this concept and a record of the thinkers who contributed to it.

3 Angus Armitage, *The World of Copernicus* (New York, NY: Mentor Books, 1956/1947), 15.
4 Margaret Mann Phillips, *Erasmus and the Northern Renaissance* (Aylesbury, UK: English Universities Press, 1964/1949), xiii.
5 Conrad Wright, *The Beginnings of Unitarianism in America* (Boston, MA: Beacon Press, 1972/1954).
6 Henry Steele Commager, *Theodore Parker: Yankee Crusader* (Boston, MA: Beacon Press, 1947), 75.
7 *Ibid.*, 83.
8 Conrad Wright, *A Stream of Thought* (Boston, MA: Unitarian Universalist Association, 1982), 111-13.
9 For more information on the central role of humanism in the history of Unitarianism see Pat Duffy Hutcheon, "The Unitarian Connection" in Michael R. Hill and Susan Hoecker-Drysdale (Eds.), *Harriet Martineau: Theoretical and Methodological Perspectives* (New York, NY: Garland Books, 2001).

6: Michel de Montaigne's Goslings[1]

The naturalism in which Unitarianism was rooted was soon almost submerged by a wave of mysticism and religious fanaticism welling up in reaction to the Renaissance. One of the few courageous thinkers who dared to stand against the tide was Michel de Montaigne of France.

Once upon a time there was a wise and brave man who warned of the dangers of mysticism in an era of cultural change and dislocation even more frightening than our own. At the risk of his very life, he argued for reason and the scientific approach to knowing. His plea and his warning are as meaningful and necessary today as they were then. The man was Michel de Montaigne, and he lived in France from 1533 to 1592.

By any measure, the sixteenth century was a dark period of history. In Europe the Renaissance had been a time of hope for humanity after the long, medieval night. Supernaturalism, magic and superstition had held sway for centuries—stamping out any tendency to apply rational, critical inquiry to human experience. However, the Dark Age had not been the first such regressive wave of anti-science to engulf Western culture. In Ancient Greece, a surge of mystical thinking in the fifth century BCE—initiated by the ideas of Parmenides and Pythagoras—had signalled the beginning of the end of the greatest flowering of thought and culture the world had ever known: the Hellenic Age. Although there had been temporary recoveries during the following centuries, by the turn of the millennium time was running out for the world view founded by the Ancients upon the premise of an orderly universe. The introduction and spread of Christianity, coinciding with the Fall of Rome and the resurgence of the neo-Pythagorean mystery cults during the Hellenistic era, resulted in the dominance of mysticism and supernaturalism for centuries to come.

And now, in Montaigne's lifetime, the naturalism of Renaissance philosophy was once again being overwhelmed by a return to supernatural absolutism and mystical and magical thinking. Religious strife was endemic. No sooner had the new Protestantism been established in Scandinavia and the north German states than it began to divide into warring factions, each with its own dogmas 'writ in stone'. In the two decades following the publication of Luther's Ninety Five Theses in 1517, heresy and witchcraft cases had mushroomed, and the mad hysteria of brutal persecutions for these alleged crimes had spread like a pestilence throughout Europe. In central Europe, John Calvin was soon rivalling in ruthlessness the Catholic Inquisition in Spain and the persecution of the Anabaptists by the Lutherans in the northeastern German states. Political as well as religious enemies of Calvin were being punished mercilessly, with burning at the stake a likely fate for those who dared to subject prevailing beliefs to the test of experience. In 1534 alone, Calvin ordered thirty-five women burned at the stake as witches, many of whom had been found guilty by no evidence other than the mystical intuitions of their accusers.

In such a climate, to support reason and scientific inquiry into moral and social matters was indeed to risk one's life. Yet there were some who dared to do so. One of the greatest of these was Michel de Montaigne.

Montaigne would not have agreed with today's New Age mystics who try to convince us that mysticism is vastly different from absolutism in religion. He saw the two stances as merely opposite sides of the same coin. All supernaturalistic doctrines, he said, spring from the same source, from our propensity to imagine that it is possible to know the unknowable. It is the yearning to experience—by mysterious means—some *immutable truth* of what is, by definition, beyond the reach of experience. Montaigne called it the ever-seductive, essentially elitist desire to be something more than human.

Referring to the population in general, he said, "They want to get out of themselves and escape from the man."[2] He recognized as particularly pernicious the religious theme expressed by the commonly heard comment: Oh what a vile and abject thing is man if he does not raise himself above humanity! "How absurd!" exclaimed Montaigne. "To make the handful bigger than the hand is impossible and unnatural. Nor can a man raise himself above himself; for he can see only with his own eyes, and seize only with his own grasp."[3]

Most worrying of all to Montaigne was the pervasive lack of interest in disciplined inquiry into the nature of the human condition, and the consequent dearth of reliable knowledge in that area. He believed that people who understand nothing about the causes of their own behaviour should not be claiming knowledge about the meaning of the cosmos. "As if he could really take the measure of anything," he said, "who knows not his own!"[4] For "man can only be what he is, and imagine what is within his reach."[5]

Mystics claim not only to *imagine* what is beyond their reach, but to *know* it in some absolute sense by an essentially mysterious means uncheckable by fellow 'experiencers'. In the face of such arrogant pretensions, Montaigne was at his ironic best. "Man is certainly crazy," he wrote, "he could not make a mite, but he makes gods by the dozens." He reminded his readers that "...for every creature there is nothing dearer or more estimable than its own being... and each relates the qualities of other things to its own qualities... Beyond this relation and this principle our minds cannot go... For why should a gosling not say thus: 'All parts of the universe have me in view: the earth serves for me to walk on, the sun to give me light, the stars to breathe their influences into me.' Now, by this same reasoning we human beings are the end and goal of which the universality of things arise."[6]

Like the goslings, humankind has tended to define the universe in its own image. Thus we imagine a transcendental Purpose, Mind and Consciousness, all clothed in man-like form. But Montaigne was implying that these are merely uniquely human attributes transferred by egoistic human beings to a universe beyond their personal comprehension. Echoing down the ages, his message anchors us in the humility of naturalistic humanism. In yet another era of burgeoning mysticism, his words serve to remind us that we are irrevocably at one with the goslings, rather than the gods.

NOTES

1 First published in *Humanist in Canada* (Winter, 1993/94), 5-6.
2 Michel de Montaigne, *The Complete Essays of Montaigne*, Trans. Donald M. Frame (Stanford, CA: Stanford University Press, 1958), 856.
3 *Ibid.*, 457.
4 *Ibid.*, 418.
5 *Ibid.*, 387.
6 *Ibid.*, 395-7.

7:   David Hume: Beacon of the Enlightenment[1]

....

A look at the extensive changes to European thought processes in the late 17th and 18th centuries and, in particular, the profound contributions of David Hume.

We sometimes think of the Enlightenment as all of one piece, but of course it was not. Like the Renaissance era preceding it, the period of radical change in world views that took place during the late-seventeenth and eighteenth centuries gave birth to a complex mix of ideas, some mutually supportable, some incompatible. For example, the roots of two conflicting modern political theories—socialism and libertarianism—were planted during the Enlightenment. Both continue to thrive in some form within humanism to this day. We can think, as well, in terms of certain more comprehensive philosophical currents of thought that came to fruition in those exciting times: currents integral to the evolution of humanism. These currents can be categorized, somewhat crudely, under the labels of *rationalism, Romanticism,* and *empiricism.* The names of three of the most influential thinkers of the Enlightenment, all of whom died in the late 1770s, have come to be associated with these currents: Voltaire with rationalism, Rousseau with Romanticism, and David Hume with empiricism.

Deistic rationalism, which represented the leading thrust of science in the Renaissance era, was reflected in the philosophical premises of Newton, Locke and numerous others, including Voltaire. Over time it had incorporated many elements of the Aristotelian axiomatic, deterministic and taxonomic approach to science that came to dominate the scholastic culture into which it had been introduced. The second major Enlightenment current—the essentially reactionary one of Romanticism—proved to have remarkable staying power. Although it can be traced as far back as the writings of Tacitus, the modern version of Romanticism originated with Rousseau's concepts of the noble savage, the General Will, and the personal 'God-within'.

Romanticism was to find a fertile seedbed in the Germanic culture, to which the Enlightenment came relatively late. A powerful early influence was the thought of Johann Gottfried Herder—the major ideologist of the *Sturm und Drang* movement. What emerged was a romantic 'cultural relativism' that rejected the Enlightenment ideals of a common humanity and universal values in order to celebrate the ideal of the German *Volk*. Hegel introduced a related version of Romantic Idealism based on a belief in an all-encompassing Spirit directing the dialectic of history. In the thought of certain other philosophers, Romanticism tended to appear as some variation of Vitalism—expressed in the notion of humankind as God.

The third Enlightenment current was remarkable in both its prescience and faithfulness to the basic tenets of Epicureanism. It was the naturalistic empiricism of David Hume. One of the most significant of the thinkers influencing Hume had been Hobbes. Another was Montaigne, who had re-introduced into the scholarly culture of the sixteenth century the works of Lucretius, along with the Epicurean philosophy that the great Roman poet had revived. During the seventeenth century Hobbes had mounted a powerful challenge to scholasticism in his emphasis on the idea that science is less a matter of abstract deduction than it is the knowledge of consequences. When like causes come under our control, Hobbes said, we see how to make them produce like effects. Hobbes was particularly critical of the dualism of Descartes. He recognized it as a major obstacle to future progress in the scientific study of humankind, in that it implied that the search for cause-and-effect relations must be limited to the non-human. In the end, the major contributions of Hobbes and Montaigne to a new way of thinking about science were: (1) their premise that humankind was as subject to cause and effect as was any other form of organic or inorganic existence; and (2) their focus on the senses as the crucial windows on experience, along with a recognition that human reason and imagination are necessarily circumscribed by what can enter those windows.

Hume incorporated all the above scientific premises into a system of explanations about two important ways in which reason functions. He maintained that the reasoning process (1) *produces* ideas by enabling the human being to generalize from regularities identified in incoming experience by the senses, and (2) *relates* these ideas by making connections among them. Such connections are based, he said, on three principles of *association*: the degree to which events are experienced as joint occurrences, their degree of recognizable similarity (or contrariety), and their apparent causal relationships (whether they are experienced as antecedent or consequent). He concluded that these principles operate both *probabilistically* and *demonstrably*. The first employs inferential logic; the second, mathematical.

Hume explained that, because reasoning on the basis of inference from experience is probabilistic, it can never achieve the certainty claimed for beliefs deduced mathematically from *a priori* assumptions or axioms. If the original experience has been inadequate or unduly selective and the generalizing faulty, factual errors can arise. This means that empiricism can never guarantee absolute truth. On the other hand, rationalism, if not conducted appropriately, can result in contradictions and absurdities. Furthermore, even where the logic is faultless, the conclusions derived by means of deduction are reliable only to the extent that the original factual premise has been precisely defined and in accordance with direct, publicly tested observation rather than imaginings. In other words, although the answers provided by deductive rationalism often provide the *illusion* of certainty, in the end that method, too, is dependent on prior generalization from experience. Thus there is no source of truth, declared Hume, that is superior and/or external to human experience.

The great twentieth-century humanist, Bertrand Russell,

has credited Hume with being the first philosopher of science to anticipate relativity and quantum physics, in that he moved beyond the limits of the old dichotomy of 'spirit versus matter' by doing away with the concept of substance altogether.[2] Hume viewed existence, instead, in terms of cause-and-effect *relations* among natural *events*. For him, scientific knowledge was a compendium of the ideas constructed by humans concerning regularities in the occurrence of such events *as experienced*. We now know that this was a step beyond the deistic determinism prevalent among scientific thinkers of the time. And that it was even more in advance of the Platonic Idealism and/or pantheism which was to undergo a popular revival in the nineteenth century. (The latter defined the 'essence' of the universe as 'spirit' or 'idea'—conceived originally in the mind of God or some other supernatural governing force.) Hume's premise has also proven sounder than that subsequently expressed by the eighteenth- and nineteenth-century materialism which viewed 'matter' as the essential and only reality, ignoring the products of mental activity.

In his famous book, *An Inquiry Concerning Human Understanding*, Hume presented one of the best cases ever made for reliance upon the empirical source of inference, as opposed to a strictly rational means of deducing proofs from *a priori* axioms. He explained that inference from experienced regularities was the sole means by which our early ancestors survived long enough to reproduce, and by which they learned from the consequences of their actions. All inference from experience, he said, is based on two powerful expectations in the sensory system: (1) that the future will resemble the past; and (2) that similar objects or events will have similar effects. He suggested that these expectations are instinctive in all forms of animal life. The imperative of survival cannot wait for the newborn to acquire experience and judgment through learning; it must rely on an inherited capacity to infer like results from like precedents. And, as learning rapidly builds on this, experienced regularities soon result in habits which are acted upon without the intercession of conscious reasoning. The most effective habits are shared by the group and eventually passed along the generations as customs. If there were no regularities to be experienced in nature, he concluded, there could be no such assumptions of cause and effect built into the nervous system by instinct and experience.[3] (Interestingly, Jean Piaget came to the same conclusion two centuries later and thought it was original with him.)

Hume was also ahead of his time in accepting no sharp distinction between means and ends. The means we choose necessarily shape our ends, he said. Unlike many of his contemporaries and most of the moral philosophers who followed after, he saw no essential conflict between the long-term good of the individual and that of the species. However, he emphasized the critical role of *reason* in instructing us on the probable tendencies of actions and the nature of their consequences—over the reaches of time and space. Here, instinct is not sufficient. In the absence of reasoning, he concluded, the drive within the individual for immediate satiation of emotional urges is indeed likely to result in actions contrary to the commonweal. He also recognized an innate human capacity for *empathy* and considered its development, through appropriate experience, to be the source of the benevolence which is necessary for morality.

While Hume was convinced that moral rules and principles are essential for group life, he did not subscribe to the prevailing Enlightenment beliefs concerning natural piety and natural justice. Rather, he concluded that morality must be assiduously taught to children from infancy on, by the adult community. In fact, he suggested that the end of all philosophical speculation must be to clarify for humankind their moral duty.(This may be why he is known as the first of the Scottish Moral Philosophers.) Morality can be a meaningful concept and desirable goal for humans only in the *absence* of beliefs in a First Cause, natural law and natural justice, according to Hume. If there were an established moral order in nature, what would human choices matter? But history teaches that injustice and tyranny are more likely than their opposites to be characteristics of nature. Precisely *because* this is the case, he declared, humans must work at developing and preserving virtue and liberty by consciously furthering empathy and the capacity to reason.[4] And, as in the study of inorganic relations and other life forms, we must learn to follow the experimental method in the study of human moral relations, he said.

Hume was adamant that the assumption of causation in human behaviour does not require acceptance of a cosmic Necessity or supernatural Purpose. He saw no justification for believing that humanity is preordained to evolve according to a set of natural laws toward some predetermined end, and even less reason to believe that we could achieve certain knowledge of such laws in the remote possibility that they do exist. In his *Dialogue with Epicurus* he was able to present his own position on religion in relative safety by putting his ideas into the mouth of his intellectual hero, and by presenting the 'cosmological' and 'ontological' proofs of God's existence from the standpoint of himself as the believing protagonist.[5] Humanists will be happy to know that Epicurus won the argument. He has Epicurus say: "You find certain phenomena in nature. You seek a cause, or author. You imagine that you have found him. You afterwards become so enamoured of this offspring of your brain that you imagine it impossible but he must produce something greater and more perfect than the present state of things."[6]

Epicurus was supposedly speaking, but the words were vintage Hume. It was such words, and the ideas carried by them, that were to spark the early scientific conjectures of Goethe, previous to his later, exclusive focus on the literary arts. They were subsequently to shape the ontological and epistemological assumptions of Charles Peirce, John Dewey, Bertrand Russell, Jean Piaget, Karl Popper and many other philosophers of naturalism— and of the modern scientific humanism based upon that philosophy. It is no exaggeration to conclude that, in the firmament of our intellectual forebears, David Hume can be counted as one of the brightest stars.

NOTES

1 First published in *Humanist in Canada* (Autumn 1998), 16-18.
2 Bertrand Russell, *Human Knowledge: Its Scope and Limits* (London, UK: Allen and Unwin, 1948), 22.
3 For an elaboration of this see Pat Duffy Hutcheon, *Leaving the Cave: Evolutionary Naturalism in Social Scientific Thought* (Waterloo, ON: Wilfrid Laurier University Press, 1996), 47-56.

4 David Hume, *An Inquiry Concerning the Principles of Morals* (Oxford, UK: Clarendon Press, 1975/1777), 172-4.

5 The Cosmological Proof of the existence of God declares that if anything exists, there must perforce exist an absolutely necessary being as its original cause. The Ontological Proof of the existence of God declares that if the idea (or 'essence') of something exists the phenomenon which that idea reflects necessarily exists as well.

6 David Hume, *An Inquiry Concerning Human Understanding* (New York, NY: The Liberal Arts Press, 1955/1728), 147.

8: Harriet Martineau: The Woman Who Thought Like a Man[1]

Readers of this collection may be wondering by now at the dearth of female landmarks along the road to reason. A telling answer is provided in the following pages. Harriet Martineau was an early nineteenth-century novelist, journalist, social reformer, educator, children's writer, philosopher of naturalism, environmentalist, social scientist and pioneering feminist who published over fifty books and almost two thousand articles and newspaper columns. During her lifetime her influence spanned North America and Europe. More than anyone, she deserves to be acknowledged as 'The Mother of Sociology'. Yet, a generation after her death in 1876 people scarcely recognized her name. This concluding section of the chapter on her life and work from the author's 1996 book "Leaving the Cave" asks, "What happened?"

The most puzzling aspect of Harriet Martineau's achievement is the response of others to it. During her lifetime she was liked, admired and even adulated by many—although the radical nature of her plainly articulated ideas aroused intermittent abuse and created numerous enemies. The odds against any woman rising to the heights of her obvious accomplishment were almost insurmountable in that male-dominated era, and her success in the face of such odds was recognized—albeit reluctantly— by most of her contemporaries. After her death, however, the chorus of calumny directed at her work and reputation rose to fever pitch, continuing unabated until, with the passage of time, her name and contributions to knowledge were buried almost as deeply as the pain-wracked body.

What was going on here? To attempt an explanation we need to begin at the beginning, with the obstacles faced by Martineau in her early years. As with all girls at that time, opportunities for formal study were virtually non-existent, while private study had to be pursued surreptitiously even in a relatively sophisticated middle-class Unitarian family such as the Martineaus. However, due to a shortage of students, Harriet was allowed to accompany her brothers to a boys' school for a brief period when she was eleven. Then, at the age of sixteen, she attended a boarding school operated by her aunt. Other than that, for the most part, she was on her own. She often spoke insightfully of the socialization into second-class citizenship to which she was subjected (although the term itself was yet to be coined). "I had no self respect," she recalled later, "and an unbounded need for approbation and affection. My capacity for jealousy was something frightful."[2] At the age of eighteen she had to get up at five A.M. in order to have time to study. When the family finances crumbled no one (least of all, Harriet) questioned the expectation that she, as the single daughter, would be the one to assume responsibility for the mother and crippled younger sister—as well as an alcoholic older brother. No one thought to chastise the mother for insisting that Harriet take on the routines and daily chores of a dutiful housekeeper and daughter, even though it meant that she could write only at night. No one wondered at the mother's refusal to allow her mature daughter to move to London, where she had a chance for regular proofreading.

During the early period of her career she was forced to deal with her mother's constant demands to live in circumstances more 'fitting to their status'. But there was no suggestion that the son James, a Unitarian minister—or the two daughters married to doctors—should share expenses. Martineau's later comment on this trying time when others were influencing her mother to pressure her into conformity was: "It was my fixed resolution never to mortgage my brains."[3] She felt compelled to write to her mother sometime later, "I fully expect that both you and I shall increasingly feel as if I did not discharge a daughter's duty, but we shall both remind ourselves that I am now as much a citizen of the world as any professional son of yours could be."[4]

And what about Martineau's experience with the publishing establishment? She seems to have been fairly treated by the editors of the Unitarian journal *Monthly Repository* which ran a number of her early essays. A little later, however, she encountered a religious publisher who appropriated her early stories and altered and used them with neither acknowledgement nor payment. This treatment was, in fact, sadly typical. She was to discover that she would invariably be resented and criticized for insisting upon the same treatment as was accorded male writers. And there was much worse. When she finally found a publisher who expressed interest in her first major project on political economy, James Mill took it upon himself to advise strongly against it, claiming that her proposed method of explaining such complex matters to the general public in comprehensible terms could not possibly succeed. When her story on the approaching overpopulation problem was published, the reviews took the form of personal attacks involving her feminine attributes. When she began to write *Society in America*, her publisher presumed that he had the right to insist that she not mention the position of women in the new United States. Later, a publisher refused to publish her novel *Deerbrook* when he discovered its characters and setting were merely middle-class. And the same man who later brought out Darwin's revolutionary book, *The Origin of Species*, broke his promise to publish Martineau's *Eastern Life* (a study of the evolution of major world religions) because of its un-orthodoxy!

The contemptuous attitude of certain particularly influential males must have been galling to an independent and proud spirit like Martineau. She met James Mill after her thirty-four-book series on political economy had become a best seller. It was just before her departure to America. He asked, patronizingly, if she intended to become an expert on that country in two years. The personally abusive outburst following her later resort to mesmerism[5] was probably also motivated largely by sexism, as it was chiefly menopausal women who were using the treatment.

This is probably the place to discuss Martineau's health problems. She was an invalid for one-third of her life. Two other women of the period, the poet Elizabeth Barrett Browning and Florence Nightingale, also wrote from their beds for many years. This raises questions about the seriousness with which female illnesses were dealt. It also forces one to consider the possibility that, for women, retiring to one's room may well have been the only way to ensure the kind of time and privacy required for concerted creative work.

Probably no autobiography before or since aroused the depth of outrage that greeted the publication of Martineau's two volumes on her life and work. She had meant it to be taken seriously, and exhibited neither false modesty nor a sufficiently acceptable 'ladylike' reluctance to express strong opinions. She also had dared to write with authority on subjects thought to be the sole preserve of men. The opinions of her expressed by some of her contemporaries are revealing. Her publisher, John Murray, intending to commend her, said that she was masculine in a feminine way. John Stuart Mill, in rejecting one of her articles, criticized the style as being what one would expect of a woman writer who had "learnt to put good women's feelings into men's words, and to make small things look like great ones."[6] (This represents a remarkable gap between precept and practice on the part of the author of *The Subjection of Women*!)

Martineau was scolded for her assertiveness, which was invariably read as conceit and arrogance. Yet, when she once tried writing under a male pseudonym she was accused of odd subterfuges that could only indicate a lack of self-confidence and an unwarranted belief that women were not taken seriously. Ralph Waldo Emerson thought her a masculine woman. Elizabeth Barrett Browning called her "the most manlike woman in three kingdoms."[7] William Howett referred to her as "one of the finest examples of a masculine intellect in a female form which have distinguished the present age."[8] Mrs. Oliphant considered her not much of a woman at all. Yet Charles Darwin was obviously entranced with her, and described how she tended to attract the brightest men in the country.

By far the worst outrage committed against Martineau during her lifetime, however, was what happened after the publication of a collaborative book entitled *The Atkinson Letters*, which comprised the correspondence between herself and a close friend, Henry Atkinson. The content was, of course, part of the problem, as it was the first time she frankly admitted to being an atheist. An amusing response was a letter to Atkinson (a virtually unknown figure compared to Martineau) advising him to publish something of his own at once "to repair the disadvantage of having let a woman speak under the same cover."[9] Far from amusing, however, was the fact that leading the attackers was her favourite brother, James—by then, a widely respected Unitarian theologian—who rushed into print with a personally insulting review. He wrote that "we remember nothing in literary history more melancholy than that Harriet Martineau should be prostrated at the feet of such a master, and should lay down at his bidding her early faith."[10] This ignorance, on the part of her most beloved brother, of his accomplished sister's long-held ideas (plus the implication that she could not possibly have come to any radical conclusion on her own) seems unforgivable. A male biographer of recent times, in recounting the incident, simply noted, "whatever the motive for his attack he did it superbly."[11]

The extremity and extent of the abuse heaped on Harriet Martineau seems inexplicable. She believed, along with John Stuart Mill, that a thinker must follow reason and evidence wherever this might lead. Yet she was almost universally condemned for demonstrating the very quality for which Mill was honoured as a man of great intellectual integrity. Both John Stuart Mill and Martineau were inheritors of certain aspects of Hume's legacy, and they lived and wrote during the same period. Both rejected Bentham's physics of morality. Mill sought to build a philosophical system based on a combination of his father's Utilitarianism, Hume's epistemology and Voltaire's idea of the sovereign individual. Martineau, while retaining the older Enlightenment notion of natural law, adopted Hume's premises about the social sources of moral-

ity and the significance of both biology and society for human behaviour—along with Hume's emphasis on the universality of cause
and effect. Most of Martineau's insights survived to become the
foundation stones of both sociology and the scientific philosophy
of Positivism, while Mill's concept of the supreme rights of the
free-floating individual lies at the roots of modern libertarianism.
On the face of it, there seems little reason for Martineau to have
been ignored for over a century, while Mill was uncritically idol-
ized. It seems we must look elsewhere for the real source and extent of the prejudice she faced.

The problem may well be that the opinion setters and
gatekeepers of her time were all men. People like her friend,
Thomas Carlyle, could have a devastating influence by dropping
comments such as "I admire this good lady's integrity and sincer-
ity; her quick, sharp discernment *to the depth it goes.*"[12] [Emphasis
added.] It was assumed that she could only spout the opinions of
her betters. For example, merely because Henry Atkinson supported the popular theory of phrenology it was widely believed
that she did also, even though she wrote carefully of her skepticism
about it.

Her project on the political economy was derided by male
intellectuals in spite of its overwhelmingly enthusiastic acceptance
and use by politicians and ordinary citizens. Her pro-democracy
study of the United States was ignored by academics who came
after, while a contemporary book far less accurate and acute in its
analyses—the pro-autocracy *Democracy in America* by de
Toqueville—has become a classic. Her scholarly *History of England* was only grudgingly acknowledged. Of the typical press response to her work, a commentator wrote that "the major reviews
tracked her progress with their usual mixture of respect tempered
with amusement."[13] A biographer, in noting her unmarried status,
makes the strange statement that "she was far too self-centered to
have made another person happy."[14] How many single male intellectuals have been characterized this way?

Even her support of women's rights was damned with faint
praise—this time by a woman. "And though women might have
wished the forerunner of their freedom to appear in a more gra-

cious guise,..."[15] she wrote. How many of the men who stood for human rights have had their contribution denigrated because they were lacking in grace? "Harriet Martineau," concluded another biographer, "was the perfect example of a limited intellect secure enough in its convictions to challenge its betters."[16] This appears as a weird *non sequitur*, following quotations that would seem to indicate quite the opposite. A similarly incongruous comment, and one equally unwarranted by the context, was that, as always, her ideas were "not less fervent for being over-simple and parochial."[17] The same prestigious biographer claimed that her writings represented an "oversimplified near-travesty of the best thought of the Enlightenment,"[18] while all of his references to her actual work would seem to indicate otherwise. Pejorative expressions like "underlying the jargon"[19] and "she sneered"[20] (by letter!) abound in this influential biography.

In describing her translation of Comte's work, the above biographer admits that "Miss Martineau's style was admirably adapted to that task, whatever the deficiencies of her mind."[21] And he concludes that "within her purpose... the book was adequate, no more."[22] This seems doubly strange given the fact that Comte was so impressed with her condensation of his theories that he had it translated back into French and substituted for his own original work in the Positivist Library in Paris. One wonders what Harriet Martineau might have accomplished if her mind had not been so deficient!

Some have said that Martineau paved the way for Marx. Certainly, she shared his passion for justice and commitment to the hope (expressed initially by Auguste Comte) of discovering immutable laws governing human nature and social change. But Martineau sought means of dispersing, rather than centralizing, economic and political power. She favoured local cooperatives for ownership of property and for managing consumption, and thought that economic production and exchange should be freer rather than more centrally controlled. In fact, the cultural transformation that Harriet Martineau inspired was to be slower and deeper than a mere surface disruption in the ownership of the means of production. Hers was a revolution not only in the values and attitudes determining our inner-most expectations about gender- and work-roles, but in the very way we perceive reality. And it was to be a long time in the making.

NOTES

1 Previously published in *Humanist in Canada* (Summer 1996), 16-19, with the permission of Wilfred Laurier University Press.
2 Harriet Martineau, *Autobiography* Vol. 1 (London, UK: Virago Press, 1877).
3 *Ibid.*, 249.
4 Vera Wheatley, *The Life and Work of Harriet Martineau* (London, UK: Secker and Warburg, 1957), 94.
5 Mesmerism (based on an early form of hypnosis) was popularized in 1778 by the Austrian 'magnetizer,' Franz Mesmer. It had undergone a comeback in the Britain of Martineau's time.
6 Valerie Sanders, *Reason Over Passion: Harriet Martineau and the Victorian Novel* (New York, NY: St. Martin's Press, 1896), 182.
7 *Ibid.*, 163.
8 *Ibid.*
9 Harriet Martineau, *Autobiography*, Vol. 11, 360.
10 Vera Wheatley, *The Life and Work of Harriet Martineau*, 310.
11 R. K. Webb, *Harriet Martineau: A Radical Victorian* (New York, NY: Columbia University Press, 1960), 300.
12 *Ibid.*, 1.
13 Valerie Sanders, *Reason Over Passion: Harriet Martineau and the Victorian Novel*, xi.
14 Janet E. Courtney, "Harriet Martineau" in *Freethinkers of the Nineteenth Century* (London, UK: Chapman and Hall, Ltd., 1920, 212.
15 *Ibid.*, 236.
16 R.K. Webb, *Harriet Martineau: A Radical Victorian*, 23.
17 *Ibid.*, 74.
18 *Ibid.*, 90.
19 *Ibid.*, 294.
20 *Ibid.*, 302.
21 *Ibid.*, 303.
22 *Ibid.*, 305.

9:   The Monistic Naturalism of Ernst Haeckel[1]

....

It is most unlikely that Harriet Martineau had ever heard of Ernst Haeckel. Had she lived to read the later works of this great thinker, she might have derived considerable hope and comfort from his valiant attempt to counter the anti-science backlash that had developed toward the end of the 19th century.

As the century drew to a close, an outstanding German scientist and philosopher was putting the finishing touches on his final offering to posterity. The man was Ernst Haeckel and the book was his 1899 *The Riddle of the Universe*. As I read his message a hundred years later I am moved to tears by his dreams for humanity that failed to materialize, and by the manner in which his message was distorted and the author maligned in the following decades. I think of what might have happened if Haeckel's words had been understood and heeded: of the lost opportunities for the human race; the possibilities unrealized; the needless cultural regression that he had hoped to forestall; and the tragic, unnecessary wars that could have been avoided. Over and over, as I read his message, I think of how different the current situation might have been if our culture had taken the road implied by Haeckel's evolutionary monism, rather than following the distorting drums of dualism and mysticism, and of the myth-based tribalisms that these world views have continued to nourish.

Ernst Haeckel (1834-1919) began his scholarly career as a physician in Berlin and soon became one of Europe's foremost scientific thinkers. As a self-styled 'child of the nineteenth century' he had been a lifetime optimist, confident that humankind was at long last about to 'leave the cave'. However, in the dying days of his century—and of his scholarly life as well—he was becoming increasingly alarmed. *The Riddle of the Universe* was a heroic, final attempt to present the scientific knowledge of his time to the reading public, and to point out the implications of this knowledge for our understanding of human behaviour.

Haeckel began by referring to "the open contradiction that has developed during the century between science and traditional Revelation"[2] and to the unfortunate fact that nineteenth-century philosophy had failed to recognize this contradiction and to incorporate the new scientific knowledge in any meaningful way. He blamed both scientists and philosophers for maintaining an "unnatural and fatal opposition between the two modes of thought."[3] He had come to believe that, compared to the remarkable advances in physical science and technology, the entire network of human social and moral organization had remained mired in a state of barbarism. And he predicted, quite rightly, that this did not bode well for the future.

Haeckel was dismayed that, in spite of all of the scientific progress to date, stupidity and superstition still reigned supreme in human culture. Everywhere, he said, revealed truths took precedence over tested knowledge. For him the culprits were the anthropomorphic dogmas of most of the world's traditional religions, and all the other dangerous delusions generated and justified by the prevailing dualistic philosophy. He saw the latter as the chief reason why so many educated people continued to grant credence to emotion and revelation over reason and observation as sources of knowledge.

His own major premise was that reliable knowledge can only be acquired through a combination of sense experience and rational thought. The philosophical position that he had developed and promoted was profoundly opposed to prevailing dualistic interpretations of the cosmos. His 'monism' was not the same thing as the nineteenth-century materialism which had been offered previously as the only alternative to the various idealisms and dualisms of the time. In rejecting the old 'matter-spirit' dichotomy, Haeckel did not follow Marx in discarding the very concept of 'spirit' or 'ideal'. His monism was, instead, in the tradition of the atomists of Hellenic Greece, and of their intellectual descendants such as Epicurus, Spinoza, Hume and Goethe, all of whom had defined spiritual phenomena as natural aspects of a universal process. For these thinkers, the human spirit was merely a product of the functioning of the human organism, emerged in a more complex form somewhat as liquid turns into vapour. Haeckel was careful to explain that his concept of spirit had nothing whatsoever to do with the erroneous idea of a specific 'vital' force—which he attributed to the writings of Albrecht von Haller. (This notion was being revived in a particularly seductive form by Henri Bergson at the very time that Haeckel was warning against it.)

Haeckel's major contributions to naturalistic thought were in the field of evolutionary science. In tracing the tragic fourteen-century black hole in the history of this study he noted that, prior to the nineteenth century, every serious attempt to explain the origin of species had been lost in what he called the "labyrinth of supernatural stories of creation." This is no exaggeration. Even the great eighteenth century Swedish taxonomist Carolus Linnaeus was still following Aristotle in believing that a given number of distinct, immutable types—each with its own immutable 'nature'—had been created by God, and that the scientist's task was merely to identify these. It is true that Rousseau, early in the same century, had dared to suggest an evolutionary kinship between humankind and the other primates. However, Haeckel noted that only Goethe had been courageous enough to point out, as early as 1775, that a distinctive formation in the jawbone of the higher apes was identical to the corresponding formation in the jaws of humans.

Johann Wolfgang von Goethe was a remarkable, complicated figure whose imagination seems to have incorporated aspects of both the empiricism and Romanticism of the Enlightenment. In his early career he did some important work in science with which Haeckel was obviously familiar, but which is seldom recognized today. Like Hume, Goethe may have been a forerunner of the philosophy of Pragmatism, in that he saw the impossibility of ascertaining the final truth of any proposition, by means of either rational or empirical criteria. Whether because of disillusionment with a scientific community that spurned his theorizing, or because he could not give up on his own personal search for a holistic approach to knowledge, Goethe then focused on literature. His powerful writings with the Romantic Idealist undertones have fascinated scholars for almost two centuries. A mark of his greatness is that, more than anyone, he inspired a virtual revolution in German culture, propelling that country, in the space of two generations, into a leadership role in literature and the arts—if not in philosophy.

In spite of giving Goethe credit for a number of prescient conclusions on the subject of evolution, Haeckel acknowledged Lamarck's 1809 treatise on the subject as the only really systematic contribution until Darwin's remarkable revolution a half-century later. In comparing these two great pioneers of evolutionary science, he said: "We find in Lamarck a preponderant inclination to deduction, and to forming a complete, monistic scheme of nature; in Darwin we have a prudent concern to establish the different parts of the theory of selection as firmly as possible on the basis of observation and experiment."[4] (He could have added that the early evolutionary concepts of Spinoza and Goethe may have actually represented a third approach: the Romantic pantheistic one in which both scientific deduction and induction tend to be superseded by a belief in the possibility of some form of holistic, direct access to 'nature's truths'.)

Haeckel neglected to mention, in this book, many of his own accomplishments. Thirty years before the discovery of the first transitional fossils he had offered a hypothesis of the lineage of human evolution that has stood the test of subsequent evidence. He suggested a remote ancestor, an ape-like primate with a relatively small brain who walked upright and used simple language. It was he who coined the phrase, 'ontogeny recapitulates phylogeny' as well as the name of 'ecology' for a new science of the diversity of life. He was also the first to employ the term 'monism' for the evolutionary perspective of a seamless web of nature existing in a hierarchy of increasingly complex, emergent forms.

However, it was on the subject of psychology that Haeckel was particularly committed to breaking new ground. He was the first to point out the significance of evolutionary theory for that "colossally confused" would-be discipline. He went so far as to declare that psychology must necessarily provide the foundation and postulate for all of the sciences, in that all knowledge is ultimately dependent on how the individual assimilates and organizes incoming sensations. He viewed psychology as the scientific study of 'the soul' (or psyche), which he defined in thoroughly naturalistic terms as the product of a functioning brain.

The problem, according to Haeckel, was that most of the psychologists of his time knew nothing about the nature and development of the human organism. They were trying to operate, as scientists, within a dualistic frame of reference that defined their very object of study as beyond the reach of science. He thought this impossible dead-end situation was due chiefly to the influence of Descartes' unwarranted conceptual separation of the human psyche from that of other animals. Haeckel also blamed the continuing popularity of Kant's philosophy—and the Medieval Christian doctrine which both perspectives had long supported. He concluded that there could be no real progress in psychology until its practitioners understood that "man's highest mental powers—reason, speech and conscience—have risen from the same faculties in our primate ancestors... [and that] his whole psychic life differs from that of the nearest related mammals only in degree and not in kind."[5]

Haeckel maintained that the concept of 'consciousness' is the citadel of the most misleading of the dominant mystical and dualistic errors found in psychology, "before whose ramparts the best-equipped efforts of reason threaten to miscarry."[6] His own view was that consciousness is simply a natural phenomenon like any other psychic product of the brain, and fully as subject to the laws of cause and effect that govern all existence. He envisaged a new 'monistic religion' that would celebrate the organic origin and the scientific and artistic achievements of human consciousness. It would be a thoroughly naturalistic one capable of guiding the course of cultural evolution in life-fulfilling directions. This is an objective with which many modern humanists might well agree. However, Haeckel did not associate monism with the term 'humanism'. In his day that term was still being used chiefly to define an orientation toward the humanities—most of which were then predominantly dualistic and Romantic in their philosophical foundations.

Haeckel's final book makes sad reading in the light of the lack of progress in philosophy and social science in the century that followed him. Nevertheless, the most tragic aspect of his story is what was happening, even as he wrote, to the evolutionary world view which he had helped to pioneer. It was already well on the way to being co-opted and perverted by a powerful current of pseudo-scientific racism. The latter had been first spelled out in an 1853 publication called *The Inequality of Human Races*, written in France by Joseph Arthur de Gobineau. Perhaps the most influential contributor to the popular distortion of Darwin's theory on which this type of polemic was based was Friedrich Nietzsche. An enemy of science as well as of religion, he transmitted the evolutionary perspective to posterity in the form of a ruthless Social Darwinism featuring the Superman and the principle that 'might makes right'. More than anything, it was the mistaken association of Haeckel's authentic Darwinian approach with this grotesque dehumanizing caricature that has prevented social science from benefiting from the remarkable progress in the life sciences that occurred during the twentieth century. The resulting anti-science prejudice at the core of social science has been disastrous for humanism as well. We can blame Nietzsche and his intellectual descendants—and the fundamentalist religious backlash that they fostered—for all the wasted decades.

NOTES

1 Previously published in *Humanist in Canada* (Winter 1998-99), 17-19.
2 Ernst Haeckel, *The Riddle of the Universe*, Trans. Joseph McCabe (London, UK: Watts and Co., 1929), vii.
3 *Ibid.*, viii.
4 *Ibid.*, 64.
5 *Ibid.*, 87.
6 *Ibid.*, 139.

10: John Dewey's Commitment to Science and Democracy[1]

....

The theories of the great American thinker, John Dewey, reflected many of the naturalistic ideas and values of Ernst Haeckel. It is unfortunate that the latter did not know of the Pragmatism being developed, even as he wrote his last, despairing book, by Dewey and his mentor, Charles Pierce. The new American philosophy was the first since Ancient times to be grounded in the concept of an all-encompassing natural existence constantly responding to the ongoing processes of evolution. During the course of his life's work Dewey jettisoned all dualisms: not only the controversial notion of 'mind' as distinct from 'matter', but long-entrenched conceptual demarcations such as 'essence versus phenomena'; 'spiritual versus material'; 'reason versus feeling'; 'fact versus value'; 'means versus ends'; 'ideal versus real'; and 'thought versus action'.

John Dewey was born in the United States the year *The Origin of Species* was published, and died almost a century later. During his lifetime he was renowned as one of the world's greatest educators and a major originator of Pragmatism—usually considered the only authentically American philosophy, and certainly the first to take evolution into account. In addition, as a pioneering interdisciplinary thinker, Dewey made significant breakthroughs in subjects as diverse as the nature of ethics, politics, education, logic, science, psychology, art and religion. This essay, written to commemorate the fortieth anniversary of his death, discusses his insights on science and democracy.

It is impossible to read the later works of John Dewey without appreciating his overriding concern for the survival of democracy. But his perceptive analysis of the crisis facing twenti-eth-century civilization, and the direction in which he saw our only hope, has been little understood—much less acted upon. It might be helpful to begin once more where he did, with a recognition of the interdependence of democracy, science and education.

Democracy, for Dewey, was never simply equated with the universal vote and secret ballot, nor with an elected and effective legislature and an opposition willing and ready to govern; nor even with the rule of law. All these he considered the *necessary* institutional features or infrastructure of democracy but, in his view, they were not in themselves *sufficient*. He was convinced that the pre-requisite for any successfully functioning democracy is a voter with the reflective habits of a disciplined scientific inquirer; and he be-lieved that the goal of education must be to develop just such habits of thought. He was referring not merely to the need to be well informed about the techniques and findings of the physical sciences, but to something much broader.

Dewey saw science as a universal approach to solving human problems, a method well-proven as a powerful tool for controlling the future ever since some curious cave man built the first fire. This led to his conclusion that the cultural requirements of science and those of democracy are so similar that one cannot survive without the other. Neither will long endure, he said, with-out people educated to doubt, inquire, observe and evaluate evi-dence; to visualize future probabilities based on accurate readings of the past and present; and to test these by precisely defined and controlled experimentation. He believed that this process would have to be applied to social matters no less than to the physical.

What brought John Dewey to the field of education was the question of how best to encourage the development of these critical habits of scientific inquiry. He was aware that much of what occurs in schools has the opposite effect. Then, as now, children were being taught to value and demand the type of answers that block the process of inquiry rather than those which empower the questioner and whet the appetite for deeper understanding. He feared that people socialized throughout childhood into a desire for certainty would never be able to function responsibly in a democratic society, no matter how much freedom was available to them. In fact, he suggested that freedom might even be counterproductive in such a case for, without intelligent and informed assessment of the probable fruits of action, widespread moral confusion and social chaos would be almost sure to result. Freedom was no more an absolute with Dewey than was any other principle for, earlier than most, he foresaw the dangers inherent in a removal of external discipline from individuals who lack the inner constraints of a reflective morality grounded in objective knowledge and values.

Dewey was convinced that science and democracy spring from the same soil. Both require freedom of inquiry and communication, the welcoming of diverse ideas, respect for logic and evidence, and awareness of the tentative nature of all knowledge. Both are instruments for the empowerment of ordinary people. Both enable individuals to participate in the control of a collective future: science through its self-corrective mechanism of rigorous public testing, and democracy by its requirement of shared decision making.

The glory of democracy, he said, is its ability to admit to the existence of problems, coupled with an institutionalized means of dealing with them. And the glory of science is the power of the method it can offer for this democratic task. Dewey concluded that the scientific way of knowing is the only reliable instrument ever invented for solving the problems posed by experience—and the most democratic. Our continuing failure to understand and act on this insight is a tragedy of monumental proportions. There is no better way to honour the memory of this great man than to recognize the problem as he so presciently defined it, and to begin the long and arduous approach to a solution.

NOTES

1. Previously published in *Free Inquiry* (Winter 92/93), 25-6.

11: The Ethical Humanism of Albert Schweitzer[1]

A Christian theologian and ethicist engages in a life-long struggle to reconcile the evidence of science and historical research with his early religious beliefs. He comes to the conclusion that philosophy and ethics must evolve along with expanding scientific knowledge; and what matters is that people adopt a world view based on 'pessimistic' assumptions about the cosmos as a source of meaning or moral guidance in conjunction with an 'optimistic' stance concerning the potential role of humans in determining the shape of the future.

Albert Schweitzer's greatest hope was to contribute to the forging of a universal morality for the troubled twentieth century. Although often defined as a Christian humanist, he actually refused to accept the limitations of any current sectarian doctrine. He believed that all religion would eventually evolve in the direction implied by the *ethical*—rather than the eschatological—teachings of Jesus; and he felt that his greatest defeat was the failure to bring Christianity along with him on this point. However, any self-defined failure of this nature was more than balanced by Schweitzer's influence on the personal morality of countless people who were privileged to know him or to read his works. The overwhelming success of this great man's life was due to the nobility and comprehensiveness of the ethical principle by which he lived. His profound reverence for life, founded on a 'will to live' and a sympathy extended to the other animals, was directed by a uniquely human respect for truth. For this alone modern humanists are well-justified in honouring his memory.

It was Schweitzer's second scholarly work, *The Quest of the Historical Jesus* (published in 1906) that propelled him into notoriety. This book presented Jesus as a man rooted in his own time and place, who saw the world in terms of then-current Jewish cultural beliefs concerning ideas about afterlife. Schweitzer's study was the most exhaustive review of the literature to date. His controversial conclusions were reached as a result of painstakingly thorough research of original sources that demolished the theological arguments for a historical Jesus as Christ and Heaven-sent Saviour of humankind. In the end, Schweitzer felt justified in asserting that Jesus "actually does belong to Palestinian Judaism and to the period to which his death is assigned."[2] He was convinced that truth must always prevail over faith and mythology, and he believed his book expressed the truth about the so-called 'Son of God'.

In Schweitzer's opinion, all theological study of Jesus since the seventeenth century had been retrograde, consisting of fruitless attempts to rationalize away the devastating evidence and conclusions of a scholar named Reimarus, who had produced "one of those supreme great works which pass and leave no trace, because they are before their time."[3] Reimarus had demonstrated that primitive Christianity—with its baptism and Lord's Supper—did not grow out of the teachings of a historical Jesus, but was created as a result of circumstances and events which occurred some time after his recorded death. Schweitzer, who began his study in the hope of disproving the Reimarus findings once and for all, ended it convinced of their truth."[My] study of the life of Jesus has had a curious history," he wrote. "It set out in quest of the historical Jesus, believing that when it had found Him it could bring Him straight into our time as Teacher and Saviour... But He does not stay; He passes by our time and returns to His own."[4] What Schweitzer had apparently found was a Jesus figure who was very much a creature of the first-century-BCE Judaic culture—shaped and limited by the eschatological beliefs of that particular region in that particular era of history.[5] His reluctant conclusion was that "the Jesus of Nazareth who came forward publicly as the Messiah, who preached the ethic of the Kingdom of God, who founded the Kingdom of Heaven upon earth, who died to give his work its final consecration, never had any existence. He is a figure designed by rationalism, endowed with life by liberalism, and clothed by modern theology in historical garb."[6]

Schweitzer did not see this as a reason for Christians to despair, however. He believed that there remains a more solid foundation for a renewed and evolving Christianity: the spirit of goodness and humanity flowing from what tradition has defined as the *ethic* of Jesus. "His spirit, which lies hidden in his words, is known in its simplicity and its influence is direct."[7] For Schweitzer it was only this ethical spirit, communicated down the generations through the minds and actions of humans, that could provide Christianity with a core of lasting value.

By this time Albert Schweitzer had arrived at a world view that recognized and accepted the probable purposelessness of the universe. Nonetheless, he was convinced that humans could create meaning and purpose in their individual lives and in their culture. His scholarly studies had persuaded him of the harm done by 'the naturalistic fallacy': the label given by the neo-Realist philosopher, G. E. Moore, to the habit of inferring what 'ought' to be from what 'is'. Schweitzer had come to realize that only humanity can supply compassion amidst raw, brutal nature; that the injection of morality into an amoral universe is the privilege and duty of our species alone. He wanted humans to stop avoiding their responsibility and guilt by wishfully projecting love and purpose into the cosmos.

Schweitzer was concerned as well with the debt owed by all members of technologically advanced societies to the exploited peoples of the globe. He recognized, long before it was popular to do so, the damage that these exploitative societies were inflicting upon the global environment by the increasingly non-viable lifestyle of their members. When an article on the needs of the Congo missions came into his hands he was ready. At the age of thirty, Albert Schweitzer decided to restructure his entire life in accordance with his principles—with the result that the story of his remarkable decades-long dedication to the needs of a developing Africa is well-recorded history.

Immediately following World War I, Schweitzer wrote *On the Edge of the Primeval Forest*, an account of his service as a doctor at the little medical outpost at Lambaréné. It was in this book that he used the now-famous phrase: "the fellowship of those who bear the mark of pain."[8] During the dark period of his internment in France as an 'enemy alien', Schweitzer had begun to think and write about the future of civilization. By the time he returned to Lambaréné in 1921, he had completed two books on the subject: *The Decay and Restoration of Civilization* and *Civilization and Ethics*. In the first of these he sketched out the results of his analysis concerning the cause of what he considered to be the current crisis of Western civilization. He included a discussion of proposals for treatment.

The problem was defined as a moral one. "If the ethical foundation is lacking, then civilization collapses, even when in other directions creative and intellectual forces of the strongest nature are at work."[9] Schweitzer explained that the ethical principles functioning as guides to society are derived from the world view prevailing in the culture at the time. If that world view does not imply that the earth is a natural and good place to be, that life is desirable and that human actions *can* contribute to progress, then civilization sinks into decadence. Schweitzer believed this had begun to occur for Western culture in the middle of the nineteenth century, *because of the failure of philosophy*. "In the hour of peril the watchman who ought to have kept us awake was himself asleep, and the result was that we put up no fight at all on behalf of our civilization."[10]

In Schweitzer's view, the Enlightenment belief that progress is immanent in nature could not survive the light shed by scientific advance. He thought that Kant had tried vainly to provide new foundations for the already obsolete eighteenth century rationalism. Those who followed after had been even more misguided, in rejecting Kant's universal Reason only to install in its place various versions of pure 'Being'. "Fichte, Hegel and others... for three or four decades succeeded in deceiving themselves and others with this supposedly creative and inspiring illusion, and in doing violence to reality in the interests of their world-view. But at last the natural sciences... reduced to ruins the magnificent creations of their imagination."[11]. Although Schweitzer admitted that much of the Romantic opposition to the older rationalism was justified,"nevertheless it remains true that it [Romantic Idealism] despised and distorted what was, in spite of its imperfections, the greatest and most valuable manifestation of the spiritual life of man that the world has ever seen."[12] Schweitzer was referring to the Enlightenment belief in human thought and reverence for truth. He was convinced that only when such ideals are reinstated, within a new and more valid world- and life-affirming world view, will there again be hope for the restoration of civilization. Schweitzer was aware that there is no ignoring the power of ideas. He noted that "Kant and Hegel have commanded millions who never read a line of their writing and who did not even know they were obeying their orders."[13]

The second of the two books published in 1923, *Civilization and Ethics*, is a scholarly treatise, equal in scope and depth to the study of Jesus. It is a survey of the evolution of world views—defined by the author as comprehensive interpretations of the cosmos—with their accompanying conceptions of the role and destiny of humanity within it. Schweitzer began with Lao-tse and Confucius, in the sixth-to-fifth century BCE, and dealt with the Indian religions, the Hebrew prophets, the early Greek Atomists, Socrates, Plato, Aristotle, Epicureanism, Stoicism and Christianity. He then moved to the seventeenth- and eighteenth-century Utilitarians; the nature philosophy of Spinoza and Leibniz and, finally, to the various Idealist philosophies of the nineteenth century. He analyzed all these in terms of the ethical stance implied and justified by them—classifying each as either optimistic or pessimistic in cosmology, and as affirmative or negative where 'world and life' are concerned.

Schweitzer explained that an optimistic cosmology attributes favourable purposes and concerns for humanity to the universe at large. A pessimistic one accepts modern scientific explanations that have discerned no conceivable plan, feelings or meaning in our inorganic surroundings. An affirming ethic postulates an active role for humans in determining their destiny, along with a commitment to life, to participation in the natural world, and to self-improvement. A negating ethic encourages the individual to despise life and withdraw from the world, which is viewed as an alien way-station en route to pure 'being' or 'salvation'. His conclusion was that only one combination of cosmic and ethical beliefs is both feasible and desirable for modern human beings. In his opinion, scientific knowledge has made it impossible for thinking people to continue believing that human progress— or some human quality such as reason or love—is in any way programmed into the universe. We must therefore accept the fact that a moral order is neither given *a priori* in, nor deducible from, the nature of the universe. Schweitzer maintained that this very fact makes the building of a sound and workable universal ethic for our species doubly necessary and potentially significant. There is no hope for progress in the creation of a more humane and life-enhancing culture unless humanity assumes the reins and provides the direction. According to him this means that the world view required for the restoration of civilization is one that is necessarily *pessimistic* in terms of expectations of cosmic morality and progress, while remaining *life-affirming* and idealistic concerning humanity's active role in its own destiny and that of the earth—its only home.

Obviously this was a difficult conclusion for Schweitzer, with his Christian background and long-held theistic beliefs, and he arrived at it only after years of honest, searching inquiry. In answer to the agonized query of "What meaning can we give to human existence, if we must renounce all pretense of knowing the meaning of the world?"[14] he warned that we have no choice but to accept the facts as science reveals them. "The hopelessness of the attempt to find the meaning of life within the meaning of the universe is shown first of all by the fact that in the course of nature there is no purposiveness to be seen in which the activities of men, and of mankind as a whole, could in any way intervene."[15] One looks in vain for morality there. According to Schweitzer, all 'holistic' views of the cosmos as the source and justification of goodness lead either to the amorality of acquiescence to the actual as predetermined; or to Nietzsche's 'will to power'; or (with Spinoza,

Fichte, Hegel and Schopenhauer) to "... the frozen sea of a supra-ethical point of view... [where] all ethical action is illusory."[16]

For Schweitzer the only way out of the morass was to have the courage to accept the universe in all its meaninglessness; to recognize that humanity possesses capacities not found in the rest of nature; and to base an ethical world view upon these capacities. "Ethics go only so far as does humanity, humanity meaning consideration for the existence and the happiness of individual human beings. Where humanity ends, pseudo-ethics begin."[17] This does not mean that concern for other forms of life is excluded, but merely that they must depend on *human* ethics to protect them.

Schweitzer believed that he was the first twentieth-century thinker to recognize that a world- and life-affirming ethical system cannot be derived from our knowledge of the cosmos, but must instead be a deliberately created product of human thought and volition. "The volition that is given in our will-to-live reaches beyond our knowledge of the world," he said.[18] He still seemed to have retained one non-negotiable imperative, however: a belief in some sort of creative life force, which he referred to as "the eternal spirit within us."[19] The task he set himself was to reconcile this belief with a world view incorporating a non-purposive cosmos. He managed this at first in a Bergsonian manner by conceptualizing the biological will to live as the manifestation, within organic life, of the eternal spirit of God. This meant that Schweitzer's position had become one of Vitalism. At this point in his intellectual evolution he had apparently satisfied himself that the premise of Vitalism was harmless, in that it need not pose an obstacle to scientific inquiry. He considered it to be the one form of dualism that, for all practical purposes, operates on the premises of naturalism.

On the other hand, Schweitzer was convinced that it does indeed *matter* for the future of humanity whether or not human beings live by a belief that the improvement of human culture is possible, and that individual choices and actions are the means to that improvement. In other words, the future of civilization depends upon the prevalence of an optimistic world- and life-affirming, ethic. And this must, of necessity, be accompanied by a 'pessimistic' interpretation of the universe: one which recognizes that we cannot look to the nature of the cosmos for guidance or responsibility in moral and ethical matters. In other words, we need "a pessimism of the intellect and an optimism of the will."

By 1960 (at the age of eighty-five) Schweitzer had finished the manuscript for *The Kingdom of God and Primitive Christianity*, although it was not published until after his death in 1965. In this book he attempted to trace the evolution of the concept of the 'Kingdom of God', from a heavenly abode to be expected in a future life beyond nature to a metaphor for an ethical condition to be realized in the hearts and minds of humans within nature. This work appears to confirm that he was moving steadily, throughout his writing life, from a position of carefully circumscribed dualism to one of outright naturalistic humanism.

Schweitzer's last book was a collection of shorter pieces entitled *The Teaching of Reverence for Life*, also published after his death. In the first essay he described the development of an ethical or moral consciousness in human culture. At the primitive level, he explained, moral concern and responsibility is limited to the family and the tribe. "The first step in the evolution of ethics is an enlargement of the sense of solidarity with other human beings."[20] Schweitzer maintained that a highly developed ethical view can be found in the ideas of Lao-tse and Confucius and in the Hebrew prophets, Amos, Hosea and Isaiah. It appeared as well in the teachings of the Brahmans, Buddhists and Hindus, and later in the words of Jesus and Paul. However, he concluded that any sense of a universal fellowship of humankind is sadly lacking in the works of Plato and Aristotle. "It remained for the Stoics and Epicureans of the second era of Greek thought to affirm the equality of all men and to take an interest in man as such."[21] The greatest prophet of humanism in the Greek world was, in Schweitzer's opinion, the Stoic, Panaetius.

After the concept of universal solidarity, the second vital element of ethics in Schweitzer's scheme is world- and life-affirmation. He considered the negation of the world, as taught by the major religions of India, classical Greek philosophy and both primitive and Medieval Christianity, to be a major obstacle to moral development in human beings. On the other hand, morality in humans is enhanced through affirmation of life and of the global environment as home to life. Schweitzer believed that this desirable ethical world view was encouraged by the ideas of the early Chinese philosophers and certain of the Hebrew prophets—as well as by the Epicureans and Stoics and, later, by Renaissance thinkers such as Erasmus and the Enlightenment rationalists.

The third prerequisite for the continued evolution of ethics is a respect for truth as the foundation of one's understanding of reality. According to Schweitzer, this leads inevitably to a rejection of any concept of the cosmos as purposeful or loving. "A philosophy that proceeds from truth has to confess that no spirit of loving kindness is at work in the phenomenal world... Ethics is not in tune with this phenomenal world, but in rebellion against it... If we attempt to comprehend the phenomenal world as it is and to deduce principles of conduct from it, we are doomed to skepticism and pessimism. On the contrary, ethics is an act of spiritual independence on our part."[22] Moreover, he noted that, even if love could be found in the inorganic universe, it is inadequate as a basis for morality. This is because "truthfulness, which is a fundamental principle of the ethical personality, cannot be deduced from it."[23]

Schweitzer's biographers found it revealing that, on the wall of his office at Lambaréné, there hung a portrait of Charles Darwin rather than one of Kant, Goethe or Luther. By this time he was, in fact, openly deploring the influence of Aristotle, claiming that the uncritical acceptance of the latter's ideas for many centuries "actually had the effect of retarding speculative and systematic thought."[24] As Schweitzer grew older it appears that he was increasingly turning to science for explanations of the universe while, at the same time, combining this scientific orientation with a growing political activism in the struggle for a non-nuclear and peaceful world.[25] He was also becoming increasingly naturalistic in philosophy, now recognizing his ultimate ethical principle, reverence for life, as a logical extension of the purely biological will to live experienced by all living beings. He saw this as requiring no violence to truth nor pedantic excursions into metaphysics, nor wishful projections of human attributes into the cosmos. Furthermore, he said, the principle permits a simple and concise definition of good and evil. "The essence of goodness is: Preserve life, promote life, help life to achieve its highest destiny. The essence of evil is: Destroy life, harm life, hamper the development of life."[26]

Schweitzer was aware that, as in the case of scientific knowledge, his proposed moral system offered no arbitrary rules or absolutes. He recognized the necessity for destroying some forms of life in some situations in order to protect and maintain other life. His solution to this recurring moral dilemma was as follows: "Each of us must decide whether to condemn living creatures to suffering or death out of inescapable necessity, and thus to incur guilt. Some atonement for that guilt can be found by the man who pledges himself to neglect no opportunity to succour creatures in distress."[27]

Albert Schweitzer's remarkable life can only be understood in the context of his ethical stance. Unlike most moral philosophers and theologians, he chose to *live* his ethics. He deliberately turned his entire life into a joyful expiation of personal and cultural guilt. Inevitably, he made less-committed people feel uncomfortable, and aroused hostility among dogmatists of every hue. Bertrand Russell tried to explain this response when he said that Schweitzer was one of those courageous people who challenged the reverences of his day.

It is clear that Albert Schweitzer was an outstanding ethicist. He provided two major additions to ethical theory. One was his insight concerning the problems created for human culture down through the ages by the dominance of idea systems uniting the optimistic cosmology common to pantheistic mysticism with a pessimistic, world-negating ethic. As he pointed out, not only is the opposite combination of beliefs desirable today, but it is the only world view both scientifically justifiable and morally imperative. Schweitzer's second great contribution was no less valuable and unique. It was his humanitarian ideal of reverence for life, and the inspiring example that he set by a long life lived in loving devotion to that principle. He liked to say Lambaréné had made it possible for him to make his entire life an argument for his beliefs.[28] Humanists who wish to understand the evolution of ethical behaviour would be well advised to heed the work of this amazing man.

NOTES

1 This is a slightly revised version of an article previously published in *Humanist in Canada* (Summer 1999), 24-28.

2 Albert Schweitzer, *The Quest of the Historical Jesus* (London, UK: Adam and Charles Black, 1954/1906), xiii.

3 *Ibid.*, 26.

4 *Ibid.*, 397.

5 See Earl Doherty, *The Jesus Puzzle* (Ottawa, ON: Canadian Humanist Publications, 1999) for a definitive modern scholarly study on this subject.

6 Albert Schweitzer, *The Quest of the Historical Jesus*, 396.

7 *Ibid.*, 399.

8 Norman Cousins, *Albert Schweitzer's Mission: Healing and Peace.* (New York, NY: W. W. Norton, 1985), 133.

9 Albert Schweitzer, *The Decay and Restoration of Civilization.* (London, UK: Adam and Charles Black, 1932/1923), vii.

10 *Ibid.*, 14.

11 *Ibid.*, 6.

12 *Ibid.*, 87.

13 *Ibid.*, 82.

14 *Ibid.*, 204.

15 *Ibid.*

16 *Ibid.*, 169.

17 *Ibid.*, 260.

18 *Ibid.*, xvi.

19 Albert Schweitzer, *Civilization and Ethics* (London, UK: Adam and Charles Black, 1949), x.

20 ——————, *The Teaching of Reverence for Life.* (New York, NY: Holt, Rinehart and Winston, 1965), 9.

21 *Ibid.*, 11.

22 *Ibid.*, 25.

23 *Ibid.*, 26.

24 Norman Cousins, *Albert Schweitzer's Mission: Healing and Peace*, 72.

25 George Marshall and David Poling, *Schweitzer: A Biography* (New York, NY: Doubleday and Co., 1975), 281-5.

26 Albert Schweitzer, *The Teaching of Reverence for Life*, 26.

27 *Ibid.*, 23

28 Norman Cousins, *Albert Schweitzer's Mission: Healing and Peace*, 124.

12: Julian Huxley: From Materialism to Evolutionary Naturalism[1]

An early 20th century British biologist followed in the footsteps of both Ernst Haeckel and his own famous grandfather in offering new insights on the nature of evolution and its implications for the study of human behaviour. He refined and expanded upon several of Thomas Huxley's key ideas, such as that of the continuity and evolutionary nature of all existence and the approach to inquiry known as agnosticism. In the process Julian explained how the 19th century scientific philosophy of materialism with its epistemology of deductive rationalism—which had distinguished earlier free thinkers from religious believers—had been rendered obsolete by Darwin's theory.

John Dewey and Julian Huxley had much in common. Both were major contributors to the building of a new, twentieth-century philosophical foundation for humanism: one which departed radically from the pre-Darwinian mix of ontological materialism and epistemological rationalism characteristic of the free thinkers of earlier times. As Huxley noted, "There are dominant systems of ideas which guide thought and action during a given period of human history, just as there exist dominant types of organisms during a given period of biological evolution."[2] He felt that, in his time, the humanist outlook was still being defined in terms of the dominant idea system of philosophical dualism, as implied by the division of reality into the 'spiritual' *versus* the 'material', or the 'sacred' *versus* the 'secular'. This was a world view which forced free thinkers into a purely deductive form of rationalism based on an autonomous, logically structured mind capable of acting upon and observing material reality from the outside, while at the same time committing them to a materialism that denied the very possibility of such a mind, as well as of the existence and causal potential of nonmaterial phenomena such as values, ideals and cultural norms.

In his lifelong commitment to furthering a more scientifically sound world view for humanity, Julian was following closely in the footsteps of his grandfather, Thomas Huxley. Thomas once remarked that "materialism and spiritualism are but opposite poles of the same absurdity."[3] As an alternative he, like Haeckel, had offered an ontology of evolutionary naturalism, although his was combined with an original approach to human knowing (or epistemology) founded on the concept of 'agnosticism'. Thomas invented this term in 1869 when, as a member of the new Metaphysical Society, he had felt the need for a name for his own philosophical position. His concept (derived from the Greek *gnosis* meaning knowledge) was to be the antithesis of 'Gnosticism': the mystical creed of an ancient Persian cult which had believed in the possibility of a mysterious, direct accessibility to ultimate truth. Thomas taught, instead, that the empirically tested facts of science are the only 'truths' accessible to fallible humans, "and *blind faith the one unpardonable sin.*"[4] In explaining agnosticism, Thomas said that it is not *what* we believe that matters so much as *why* and *how* we believe it. "Moral responsibility lies in diligently weighing the evidence. We must actively doubt; we have to continually scrutinize all our views, not take them on trust."[5]

What Thomas Huxley was attempting with his new concept was to switch the emphasis from the specific *content* of the beliefs that humans hold (whether these beliefs acclaim or disclaim the existence of something) to the *process* by means of which people attain and retain them over time. For him, agnosticism was "not a creed, but a method, the essence of which lies in the rigorous application of a single principle... It is the fundamental axiom of modern science... Do not pretend that conclusions are certain which are not demonstrated or demonstrable."[6] He was, in fact, changing the emphasis to the scientific method of inquiry, with all its strengths and limitations, as the sole source of reliable knowledge. However, his concept was much misunderstood, even by supporters, and to this day many humanists tend to write off agnostics as people who merely refuse to take a stand on the question of theism.

Other concerns of Thomas Huxley involved efforts to convince his fellow Darwinists that free thought does not necessarily imply free sex; and that because non-human nature is lacking in a moral order this does not mean humans are destined to operate according to the laws of the jungle. But perhaps his most original—although generally unrecognized—conceptual breakthrough is to be found in the following musing concerning what many theorists now consider to be the role of complex, dynamic, adaptive systems in evolution. "Evolution... first adumbrated in solar astronomy, then clearly evident in embryology and paleontology, a principle of development discernible in chemistry and obviously fundamental to the study of all terrestrial life... has progressed from very simple to increasingly complex forms, producing consciousness, intelligence and morality as *emergent* values along the way."[7] [Emphasis added.]

With such a background it is not surprising that, some four decades later, Julian Huxley came to feel that the time was then long overdue for a radical restructuring in world view to match the new paradigm that Darwin had forced upon biology. He decided to devote his life to completing the revolution in social thought instituted by his grandfather and Ernst Haeckel—and by the Pragmatists. He proposed that the new world view be one of Evolutionary Humanism. In explaining this perspective Julian looked to Pragmatism. He used William James' comprehensive term 'world stuff' to replace the more restrictive concept of 'matter'—which he considered to have been thrown into question by the new physics. Matter or substance as the basis of reality had previously been soundly repudiated (along with dualism) by Bertrand Russell, so Huxley was in good company. The fact that, in 1957, the British free thinkers changed the name of their journal from

The Rationalist to *The Humanist* provides us with some evidence of Julian Huxley's success in spreading the new ideas.

Julian was a far more innovative thinker than is generally recognized today, even by humanists. Although he was one of the foremost biologists of his time, his most important contributions had to do not primarily with genetic evolution but with that of culture, and with the interrelationships between the two processes. Today we are growing accustomed to the concept of interactive, feedback systems; and to scientists at the forefront of physics, engineering, neuro- and cognitive-psychology and evolutionary science conceptualizing their theories in terms of these. But few of the people concerned are aware that it was Julian Huxley who laid much of the groundwork for this type of thinking. He did this by spelling out the critical evolutionary role of 'emergence': the concept first applied to evolution by his grandfather and further refined by the Pragmatist George Herbert Mead.

In fact, the development of this key concept is itself an excellent example of how components of culture evolve. John Stuart Mill is actually credited with introducing the idea of 'emergence', while the philosopher of science George Henry Lewes and the psychologist Wilhelm Wundt both subsequently built on it.[8] However, Mead, who read Wundt as a student in Germany, appears to have been the first to recognize the significance of 'emergence' for an interdisciplinary evolutionary theory. There appears to be a direct line from his writings to Julian Huxley's remarkably prescient conjectures about the process by which an accumulation of quantitative changes could somehow set the stage for the triggering of a seemingly qualitative transition in the nature of patterns of interaction, and the units involved in these. And, of course, all of this is now supported by today's chaos theory—appropriately understood—with its implications for change at the more complex levels of the evolutionary hierarchy.

Julian Huxley viewed the breakthrough into symbolic language and culture, experienced so far by only one branch of upright primates, as the most significant example of emergence. As he explained it: "The critical point in the evolution of man—the change of state when wholly new properties emerged in evolving life—was when he acquired the use of verbal concepts and could organize his experience into a common pool."[9] The mental processes resulting from this transition are what people mean when they speak of 'mind'. However, he noted that, "mind is not an entity in its own right, and our minds are not little separate creatures inhabiting our skulls. So it is much better to speak of 'mental activities', though 'mind' may be used as a shorthand term."[10]

Huxley went on to argue that the philosophical basis of the older materialism is totally undermined by the fact that a high degree of mental organization could only have come about if it conferred survival advantages on its possessors; in other words, if it operated as an objective, feedback *causal* force in the real world. Materialism, he pointed out, denies the effective reality of mental processes and their products, such as ideas and norms and customs. He even went so far as to devise terms to symbolize the products of mental activities within the individual as well as those cultural products resulting from, and communicated by, groups of people interacting and sharing and testing their ideas. His name for the first category was 'mentifacts', and for the second, 'socifacts'.

A major reason for the lack of appreciation of Julian Huxley's work is the misinterpretation and misrepresentation of his ideas that became prevalent in mid-century and has continued to this day. He was often called a dualist by people who saw his repudiation of philosophical materialism—and his occasional use of terms such as 'mind', 'ideals' and 'spiritual'—as evidence that he believed in some sort of demarcation between these non-physical attributes and the more concrete aspects of existence. But Huxley recognized no such split in the 'world stuff'—or interaction of mass and energy—comprising nature. In response to those who argued that it was Marxist *materialism* that had actually pioneered the view of reality as only one process or substance, Julian had a telling reply. "Marxism," he said, "accomplished a curious feat: it took over the basic dualism of Western European thought, but then proceeded to transform it into a phony monism, a sham unitary system, by denying validity to one of its components, namely the mental aspect."[11]

Julian Huxley was perhaps the first evolutionary theorist to recognize the reality and causal significance of human society and culture: a reality which materialism—by the very nature of its premises—is forced to ignore. He concluded that in the future it would be cultural factors, rather than biological, that would determine the direction of evolution. He saw human culture as unique in the world, in that "it enabled life to transcend itself, by making possible a second mechanism for continuity and change in addition to the genetic outfit in the chromosomes. This is man's method of utilizing cumulative experience, which gives him new powers over nature and new and more rapid methods of adjustment to changing situations."[12]

Julian Huxley has often been criticized for his position on eugenics. He did indeed believe that humans, with their newly acquired powers, must accept responsibility not only for the kind of culture transmitted to following generations, but for the health of the gene pool bequeathed as well. He was aware, earlier than most, that our new technologies were providing us with formidable tools for interfering with the process of natural selection which had given our species its current adaptive capacities. He felt that a high level of technical expertise in the hands of people still mired in a world view rooted in mysticism and superstition made for a dangerous situation. This impelled him to sound a warning concerning the direction in which the mindless use of technology might propel us, and the kind of destructive genes that we might be causing to multiply in our own species and in others, by our shortsighted behaviour.

Huxley has also been accused of merely rehashing the Vitalism and belief in essential Progress characteristic of the theories of Albrecht von Haller and Henri Bergson. But, while it is true that Julian—like the Pragmatists before him—built on certain of Bergson's insights about the evolution of self-consciousness, those particular ideas were not predicated upon Vitalism. They were grounded, instead, in the then-crude and revolutionary concepts of 'hierarchy' and 'emergence' in evolution. Julian explained the emergence of self-consciousness solely in terms of the self-transforming nature of evolution. He claimed that the psycho-social-cultural level of interaction, although different in quality from the inorganic level, has its total source within the latter. In a similar way, life itself differs from non-life, but has evolved solely out of the inorganic substance of the cosmos, with no vital force acting from outside the process. "To postulate a divine interference with these exchanges of matter and energy at a particular moment in the earth's history is both unnecessary and illogical," he concluded.[13]

As for Julian Huxley's belief that evolution is progressive in nature, he did employ the concept, but in a carefully defined and limited way. His writings make it clear that he viewed evolutionary advance solely in terms of the accumulation of improvements in effectiveness resulting from increasing complexity and diversification of organization. As he explained it, "We need a term for the sum... [of these accumulations] through the whole of evolutionary time, and I prefer to take over a familiar word like progress instead of coining a piece of esoteric jargon."[14] In fact, it was his evolutionary approach to language, and his consequent preference for using everyday words while wresting them from their dualistic framework and redefining them in monist terms, that is responsible for common misunderstandings of two of Julian's other key concepts: the 'ideal' and the 'spiritual'. In the latter cases, he was attempting to present a comprehensive *naturalistic* explanation for all those shared human experiences and strivings and collective memories which, although clearly not physical, must be recognized as objectively real because they have observable causes and effects. (It is for just such a reason that we recognize the existence of atoms and neutrinos.)

Long before Edward O. Wilson wrote about consilience, Julian Huxley was maintaining that humankind must attempt to achieve a unity of knowledge. According to him: "Since the only potentially universal type of knowledge is scientific in the broad sense of resting on verified observation or experiment, it follows that this unity of knowledge will only be attained by the abandonment of non-scientific methods of systematizing experience, such as mythology, superstition, magico-religious and purely intuitional formulations."[15] He then went on to list the most important ideas on which the unified system must be based. These were: (1) the unity of nature, as opposed to all forms of dualism; (2) all nature as process, to be explained by evolution rather than any static mechanism; (3) evolution as directional, but only in the sense that it generates greater variety, complexity and specificity of organization—even though this may lead into dead ends; (4) evolutionary advance as defined in terms of the realization of new possibilities in nature; and (5) an evolutionary view of human destiny, with humankind recognized as the chief instrument of further evolution, as against all theological, magical, fatalistic or hedonistic views of destiny.

Julian was not optimistic about the possibility that his objective of a unitary approach to knowledge would be realized. He was all too aware of the prevalence and staying power of dualism. "The very organization of our language, and all our habitual ways of thinking," he wrote, "artificially dissociate real and ideal, object and subject, quantity and quality, material and spiritual,...'we' of the in-group and 'they' of the out-group, individual and society, intuitional appreciation and intellectual analysis. How can we expect people to grow up whole in a world which is presented to them already split by organization of thought, and when the main instrument we give them in education is one for carving reality into separate slices?"[16] This is why he was so committed to cleansing ordinary language of its dualistic connotations—not by refusing to use the bulk of the terminology so firmly rooted in the culture (as if that were possible), but by working at redefining the concepts signalled by the familiar terms and thus contributing to the process by which language has inevitably evolved throughout human history. It is ironic that his reward for this heroic attempt was to become the object of attack not only by those who sought to preserve the 'sacred', but by many 'secularists' as well.

NOTES

1 Previously published in a somewhat shorter version in *Humanist in Canada* (Autumn 1999), 28-31.
2 Julian Huxley, *Essays of a Humanist* (London, UK: Chaffo and Windus, 1964), 51.

3 Adrian Desmond, *Huxley* (London, UK: Penguin Books, Ltd., 1997), 319.

4 *Ibid.*, 345.

5 *Ibid.*, 75.

6 William Irvine, *Apes, Angels and Victorians* (Cleveland, OH: The World Publishing Co., 1955), 321.

7 *Ibid.*, 340.

8 David Stover and Erika Erdmann, *A Mind for Tomorrow* (Westport, CT: Praeger, 2000), 86.

9 Julian Huxley, *Evolution in Action.* (New York, NY: Mentor Books, 1953), 115.

10 *Ibid.*, 76.

11 Julian Huxley, *Knowledge, Morality and Destiny* (New York, NY: Mentor Books, 1957), 233.

12 *Ibid.*, vii.

13 Julian Huxley, *Evolution in Action,* 20.

14 *Ibid.*, 99.

15 Julian Huxley, *Knowledge, Morality and Destiny,* 48.

16 *Ibid.*, 239.

13: Sartre and Camus on Existential Humanism[1]

These two articulate thinkers of the post-war period have had a powerful impact on several generations of university-educated young people. The world views of both writers were irrevocably shaped by Existentialism, with its rebellion against science as well as religion, and its key assumption of the 'absurdity' of the human condition and the meaninglessness of life. However, Camus spent most of his brief writing life analyzing and criticizing—rather than supporting—the popular philosophy, while Sartre was to push its premises to their ultimate 'absurd' and 'meaningless' extremes.

Huxley had been trying to present an alternative not only to the older materialism and rationalism, but to a newly popular current of thought which blossomed immediately after World War II. This was Existentialism: a somewhat incompatible set of ideas taken from the writings of Karl Marx, Sören Kierkegaard, Friedrich Nietzsche, Henri Bergson, Edmund Husserl, Fyodor Dostoyevsky, Karl Jaspers and Martin Heidegger, among others. It was the works of these writers that dominated the university humanities departments of the day. Not surprisingly, a host of former students came of age entranced with the ideas of these men, and knowing little of alternative world views. Among the products of such universities were Albert Camus (who had come to France as a young graduate from Algiers) and Jean-Paul Sartre.

With the advent of peace, Sartre had been quickly propelled into the role of 'prophet of the new order'. This was initially due to his rise to international prominence in the latter days of the war as a journalist for Camus' clandestine Resistance journal, *Combat*. Then, in the Fall of 1945 he spoke on "Existentialism and Humanism" to a record crowd at the *Club Maintenant* and became an instant celebrity. He began to publish the journal *Les Temps Modernes* and was soon writing novels and philosophical treatises as well. Altogether, Sartre's published works were to exert a powerful and lasting impact on several generations of philosophers, creative writers and social scientists.

Camus became known chiefly for his Existentially based novels. He also published collections of thoughtful essays on the popular new philosophy—agonizing about its internal contradictions and debatable implications for human morality. Both writers contributed to the creation of an anti-science version of humanism that is still strongly influencing members of the humanist community, especially in Europe. And the theory informing their world view is one of the major sources of the 'postmodernism' so popular throughout academia today. Perhaps it is time to attempt an assessment of the influence of Sartre and Camus, now that civilization has emerged from the troubled twentieth century which these famous Existentialists did so much to shape.

A Revolutionary Philosophy

What seems to have appealed to Camus and Sartre, and to many of their contemporaries who came of age in France and Germany during the inter-war period, was a profoundly pessimistic and life-negating world view. Schweitzer (the cousin of Sartre's mother) had chosen to spend his lifetime struggling to reconcile the concept of a morally meaningless universe with personal life-affirmation. However, the generation following him were not interested in launching on this journey. They had forsaken the older faith in God and in a purposeful cosmos, while continuing to hold fast to the belief in human powerlessness dictated by traditional religion. In spite of being mired at this halfway point, they imagined they were rebelling against *all* of the belief systems of their parents: religious as well as political. Strongly influenced by Marxism, this generation of youth had accepted the atheism of that revolution-ary movement while rejecting its optimistic prophecy for the sal-vation of humankind. For young European intellectuals of the post-war era, the Enlightenment ideals of reason and objectivity were merely bourgeois justifications for imposing a false order on the inevitable chaos of existence. Like the postmodernists of today, they were strongly attracted by the concept of chaos. They be-lieved it somehow supported their belief in limitless freedom even though, for them, the prospect of that condition inspired more anxiety than hope. This was the world view of the gifted Jean-Paul Sartre and Albert Camus, whose writings were to give voice to the fears and ideals of rebellious youth for decades to come.

In many ways that voice was a lonely and despairing one. Camus, in agonizing about his own intellectual plight, put it clearly. "A world that can be explained even with bad reasons is a familiar world. But in a universe suddenly divested of illusion and lights, a man feels an alien, a stranger. His exile is without remedy since he is deprived of the memory of a lost home in the hope of a promised land."[2] Unlike those, such as Sartre, who were un-questioningly committed to the new philosophy, Camus never ceased to worry about many of its assumptions. Although disillu-sioned with science because it offered only hypotheses rather than the certainty he craved, he was nonetheless uneasy about the anti-rational nature of Existentialism. "Never perhaps at any time," he noted, "has the attack on reason been more violent than in ours."[3] He even went so far as to accuse the popular philosophy of creat-ing its own new gods in the process of rejecting the old ones. One is not sure, however, whether he is with the Existentialists or against them when he muses: "Through an odd reasoning, start-ing out with the absurd over the ruins of reason, in a closed uni-verse limited to the human, they deify what crushes them and find reason to hope in what impoverishes them."[4] He even called the Existential attitude philosophical suicide, adding that "for the ex-istentials negation is their God...[and] that God is maintained only through the negation of human reason."[5]

We can sympathize with Camus in his identifying of a host of negations from which the new philosophy had sprung, and in his suspicion that Existentialism offered little that was positive to replace the rejected certainties. In fact, the unanswerable questions raised by its followers were legion. For example, they agonized over the issue of whether human beings are incapable of forging a humane morality, in the absence of an unalterable 'Good' beyond the universe of nature. They seemed to believe that humanity's new-found freedom from an immanent necessity was the result— not of a knowledge-induced change in our view of reality, but of an actual alteration in the 'essential' conditions of existence. What if God *had existed* in the past as the ultimate source of moral laws and cosmic purpose, they wondered, but is *now dead*? What if human freedom is not something long-present and only-now-discerned but, instead, represents an abrupt abandonment of His Creation by a dying Creator? In that case humankind would be condemned to meaninglessness and chaos, rather than being released from the fetters of the cave of past ignorance. Indeed, this was the conclusion of most of the disillusioned former 'true believers' who were drawn to Existentialism—as distinguished from authentically unfettered thinkers such as a Martineau, Haeckel, Dewey or Huxley.

If Camus saw all this so clearly, why did he continue to associate himself with Existentialism? Susan Sontag, in considering this question, arrives at the following conclusion:

> Being a contemporary, he had to traffic in mad men's themes: suicide, effectlessness, guilt, absolute terror. But he does this with such an air of reasonableness, measure, effortlessness, gracious impartiality, as to place him apart from the others. Starting from the premises of a popular nihilism, he moves the reader—solely by the power of his own tranquil voice and tone—to humanist and humanitarian conclusions in no way entailed by his premises.[6]

It may well be that Camus was able to identify himself as both an Existentialist and a humanist only by adding logic to the list of rejected attributes entailed in the philosophy. He wrote a number of books of essays and incredibly moving novels, all in a tone of alienation and passionate rebellion combined with a revulsion against nihilism and all forms of violence. Although he never seems to have addressed Sartre directly, one cannot help but feel that his message was directed at his former friend, who epitomized much that Camus himself had come to fear and abhor in the new world view. For Sartre, it was always Martin Heidegger's version of Existential-Phenomenology (introduced to him by his Nazi captors during his brief and comfortable period of internment at the onset of the Occupation) that exerted the most powerful influence. For Camus, on the other hand, Heidegger represented all that he resisted and feared both in the German culture of the time and in Existentialism.

The Quest for Certainty

Perhaps it was their contrasting experiences in war-time France that started the two thinkers down their very different post-war roads. Camus' years of underground work in the Resistance are clearly reflected in his moving "Letters to a German Friend" in the book, *Resistance, Rebellion and Death*. "We are fighting", he wrote then, "for the distinction between sacrifice and mysticism, between energy and violence, between strength and cruelty; and for that even finer distinction between the true and the false."[7]

Sartre, who had accommodated quite happily to the Occupation, saw things rather differently. He felt that Heidegger's perspective could be readily reconciled with his own anti-scientific and intuitional notion of truth, and to his 'discovery' of contingency. Sartre's notion of contingency was very different from that developed earlier by the Pragmatists, however. Whereas they had recognized an element of chance in the human process of choice— within the context of a universe of causally related events—Sartre rejected cause and effect entirely. Contingency, for him, was never the feedback causality of Darwin and the Pragmatists, nor even the probabilistic indeterminacy recognized by David Hume (and Democritus so long before). For Sartre, the entire concept of causality was nothing more than an abstract fiction of positivistic 'scientism'. When pressed to define his own notion of contingency he explained it as merely, "To be there, without rhyme or reason, necessity or justification; it is to exist without the right to exist".[8]

Sartre was committed to the notion of 'the intentional act'

(as developed by Edmund Husserl, the founder of Phenomenology)[9] and he combined this with a Transcendentalist belief in intuition as the source of absolute knowledge. He had rejected Husserl's neo-Kantian idea that knowledge about external reality is determined by universal logical structures within the human mind: structures antecedent to all experience. In a tragic distortion of both Marxism and Pragmatism, Sartre proclaimed that *existence precedes essence*. However, he meant by this not the public testing of hypotheses through action with which the earlier philosophers had associated *praxis*. He interpreted the expression to mean, instead, that individuals formulate essential truth out of their own actions by subjectively assigning meaning to their experience in the process of creating it.

In spite of a lifetime of rebellion, Sartre was never able to break out of the idea system into which he had been socialized from birth: that of a dualism separating the phenomenological *process* of existing from some Platonic *meaning* or 'essence' of existence. In the end, his radical rejection of the *status quo* in philosophy turned out to be the equivalent of Marx's rejection of Hegelianism. Without questioning the basic premise, Sartre simply reversed the temporal sequence, or causal relationship. His 'existence precedes essence' represented no real breakthrough into naturalism or evolutionary thought—as had John Dewey's similar claim that 'action precedes thought'. Sartre differed fundamentally from the Pragmatists in that he continued to assume the possibility of 'essential' truth. However, for him, this truth was to be found neither by means of the empirical positivism of the Realist nor the deductive logic and 'coherence test' of the Idealist. It was, instead, a private creation of the acting subject.

Camus wrote of truth as well, but with more humility. "What is truth?" he asked rhetorically in a letter to a former German friend—no doubt a philosopher. "To be sure [this poses a problem] but at least we know what falsehood is; that is what you have taught us... What is man?... He is the force of evidence. Human evidence is what we must preserve."[10] Camus, in spite of his Existentialism, seems to have been an empiricist at heart. Sartre, on the other hand, although committed to building a radical epistemology, was so irrevocably embedded in the conceptual framework of neo-Platonism that he believed the very notion of universally applicable categories demanded the premise of their pre-existence as 'forms' in the mind of God. This made him unable to distinguish between the Kantian idea of *a priori* logical structures and those quite different humanly created general categories of thought known as scientific: empirically derived concepts reflecting regularities in the shared experience of the human group, as communicated, tested and transmitted across and down the generations by living people.

For example, Sartre often referred to the idea of 'human nature' as a term defining the immutable nature of man; and he rejected this. "Thus there is no human nature, as there is no God to conceive it."[11] But the possibility that there might be similarities in the biological makeup and sociocultural experience of the human species justifying the use of general explanatory constructs escaped him utterly. His metaphysical assumptions implied no possibility of objectivity *other than* that defined by Platonic universals existing as transcendent logical forms amenable to grasping by the human mind. Because this premise was obviously in conflict with his Existential theory of knowledge, Sartre concluded that the goal of objectivity itself had to be jettisoned.

Me and the Other

Sartre's confused thinking on the requirements of objectivity is not out of character. Even concepts most basic to his theory remain ambiguous throughout his written works. Sometimes he seemed about to explain something clearly, but he invariably stopped short. For example: "Subjectivism means, on the one hand, freedom of the individual subject and, on the other, that man cannot pass beyond human subjectivity."[12] However, he did not reject the first meaning. He merely claimed that the second was the *deeper* meaning of Existentialism. But this does nothing to clarify his position. What we need to know is his answer to the question of whether the individual can pass beyond *personal* subjectivity. In other words, is intersubjectivity possible within the framework of Sartre's Existentialism?

Sartre did not even acknowledge this question as a problem. The sharing and checking of personal experience was not his goal. He simply did not regard it as necessary. For him, Marxist theory was the only possible source of 'concrete knowledge'. However, he maintained that, within the Marxist frame of reference, "the questioned and the questioner must become one."[13] In other words, knowledge can only be gained by the subjective route, even though the answer arrived at will inevitably be the 'objective' one dictated by Marxist premises. In Sartre's opinion, to try for a disciplined, publicly tested objectivity is to be 'scientistic' or 'intellectualist'—both undefined but obviously very bad things to be. For Sartre there was no need to achieve intersubjectivity for the purpose of testing the reliability of one's conclusions against the experience of others. One need only seek to comprehend the "object's *situation* in relation to the social whole and its totalization inside the historical process."[14] It seems clear that Sartre simply never questioned his own Marxist infallibility nor that of his mythical subject.

Sartre saw intersubjectivity merely in terms of the subject discovering others "as the condition of his own existence. He recognizes that he cannot be anything... unless others recognize him as such."[15] According to him, one is aware of the existence of others in their role of enhancing one's own being, and *only* in that role. But the intent of the subject is to resist possession so as to complete its own creation. "Thus my project of recovering myself is fundamentally a project of absorbing the Other."[16] Presumably, the more I can absorb of the Other and of what Others have absorbed of me, the less tenuous is my self-creation. Ferocious and irreconcilable conflict is therefore a fundamental condition of existence between Me and the Other. For Sartre the sexual relationship was the classic example of this. Such was the nature of his intersubjectivity—and of his approach to women as well!

Existentialism and Marxism

Although Sartre always proclaimed that the *practical* aspects of his philosophy were all-important, he would probably want to be remembered most for his *theoretical* reconciliation of Existentialism and Marxism. He believed that he had accomplished this by bringing the subject as a project creator into the 'totalizing' activity of the dialectic of history. This required accepting the Marxist premise that humans do not create themselves from nothingness but, rather, out of the raw materials of the concrete historical epoch that has been, so to speak, thrown off the flywheel of the dialectic. It also necessitated giving up the Existentialist idea of a meaningless and chaotic universe and accepting the Marxist dialectic as the sole source of meaning and order in human history. But Sartre broke from Marxist thought in insisting that the *praxis of individuals* will complete the epoch's 'totalization', out of which synthesis new contradictions will emerge.

Sartre's personal synthesis of the two opposing theories also required an admission by traditional Marxists that the precise nature of future epochs and the process by which they are totalized are not immanent laws of history and hence discoverable by objective science but are, instead, indeterminate and must be comprehended subjectively as a condition of perpetual action and creation. "The investigator must, if the unity of history exists, grasp his own life as the Whole, the Part, and the link between the Parts and the Whole, and as the relation of the Parts among themselves, in the dialectical movement of unification. He must be able to make the leap from his own singular life to History."[17]

One comes to see one's own life, and that of the Other, as a microcosm of society, the meaning of which will be revealed in the "dynamic relations of the different social structures, insofar as they are transforming themselves through History."[18] The group, as such, is called into being through the actions of subjects, as they locate it "in relation to the social order and the totalization of the historical process."[19] Sartre explained that the questioned and the questioner will thus have become one, and Marxist thought will have given up its scientism. While continuing to provide the universe of meaning for all sociological and anthropological knowledge, it will have accepted Existentialism as its true foundation and only method.

Meanwhile, Camus had arrived at very different conclusions about Marxism. He believed that Communism had been doomed from the start, because it had inherited "a definition and doctrine that pictured freedom as suspect,... [with the result that] as the revolution little by little became stronger, the world's greatest hope hardened into the world's most efficient dictatorship."[20] When accused of merely needing to reject the optimism offered by doctrines of salvation (whether of the theological or ideological variety) Camus had this to say: "By what right could a Christian or a Marxist accuse me of pessimism? I was not the one to invent the misery of the human being or the terrifying formulas of divine malediction. I was not the one to shout for the damnation of unbaptized children. I was not the one who said that man is incapable of saving himself... and his only hope was in the grace of God. And as for the famous Marxist optimism! No one has carried distrust of man further; and, ultimately, the economic fatalities [that it predicts] for this universe seem more terrible even than divine whims."[21]

The permanent break between Camus and Sartre came in 1952, when Camus denounced Stalin and took a stand against violence. Sartre remained a committed propagandist for Stalin's Communism, returning from a trip to Russia in 1954 waxing ecstatic on the 'fact' that he had found total freedom for criticism in the U.S.S.R. Even the violent quelling of the Hungarian Revolution left him unwavering, although the Prague Spring finally caused his faith to crumble. From then on, his revolutionary enthusiasm was directed chiefly to the Algerian struggle for independence, the Paris Student Uprising and the Castro revolution in Cuba.

The Role of Violence

Given these interests, it is not surprising that one of Sartre's philosophical projects was an attempt to refine and extend the Marxist justification of violence as the means of bringing about change in society. He saw violence as being *subjectively* as well as objectively necessary, in that it results from the inevitable scarcity of resources in relation to human needs. He explained that social relations in each epoch are relations of reciprocity modified by scarcity. Each person is simultaneously revealed as both a potential survivor and a potential 'expendable', depending upon which group has access to power. This means that conflict is unavoidable, as is violence and inhumanity. "For each person, man exists as *inhuman* man, or... an alien species... Each person *is* the inhuman man for all the Others; he considers all the Others as inhuman man; and he really treats the Other with inhumanity."[22] Each person exists for the Other as the threat of death, and the choice to kill becomes the ultimate creative, and therefore moral, act. As Sartre put it, "the ethical reveals itself as a destructive imperative: evil *must* be destroyed... Violence claims always to be *counter* violence, that is, retaliation for the violence of the Other."[23] Sartre and his followers seem to have been unaware of how much all this resembles the brutishly tyrannical state of nature that Hobbes recognized as inevitable in the absence of authority structures of some kind.

Sartre concluded that, for much of the time, this urge to violence is held in abeyance, as social relations persevere in the 'practico/inert field'. But at some particular stage in the 'totalization' of an epoch, the exploited fuse into a condition of solidarity, and act as one against the exploiters—now recognized as the group Other.

> The essential characteristic of the group in fusion is the sudden restoration of freedom... It has become, in the practico/inert field, the mode in which alienated man must live his own servitude in perpetuity, and finally, the sole means he has to reveal the necessity of his alienation and his powerlessness. The explosion of the revolt, as liquidation of the collectivity, does not directly draw its sources from the alienation, revealed by freedom, nor from freedom suffered as powerlessness; a conjunction of historical circumstances is needed; an historical change in the situation; a risk of death, violence.[24]

Although Sartre's writing on this subject is ambiguous, one can only conclude that he considered violence as both essential to humanity's creation of itself and a necessary part of a society's revolutionary birth pains. An explosive combination indeed!

In stark contrast to all this, Camus often expressed horror at the violence implied in the philosophy as developed by Sartre and others. It was for this reason that he refused to take sides in the revolt in his Algerian homeland. He viewed all resort to violence to achieve political ends as *murder*, pure and simple. He saw it as integrally related to nihilism and rejected both. According to him, philosophies that accept nihilism and violence usually arrive at those questionable ends because of an initial commitment to either *absolute freedom* or *absolute justice*, neither of which is feasible in civilized society. Camus believed that absolute freedom amounts, in the end, to the right of the strongest to dominate; while absolute justice can only be achieved by the suppression of all contradiction and creativity—a course ultimately destructive of freedom as well. His own credo and hope for the future was expressed as follows: "The rebel rejects divinity in order to share in the struggles and destiny of all men... The earth remains our first and last love. Our brothers are breathing under the same sky as we; justice is a living thing... Each reminds the other he is not God and that this is the end of Romanticism."[25]

Significance for Humanism

The preceding message, as expressed by Camus, comes across as profoundly humanistic. What, then, of *Sartre's* claim to be a champion of humanism? If his work has anything of lasting value it would have to be the focus on individual choice and the idea that we are responsible for what we do with our lives—viewpoints typical of Camus as well. Sartre also shared with Camus an emphasis on subjective experience as the *starting point* for all knowledge. This may have served as a helpful antidote to the continued prevalence of systems of thought impervious to the test of experience. But both ideas, in the form expressed by Jean-Paul Sartre, carried with them some extremely misleading baggage. Individual freedom to choose can only be respected and protected if both its consequences for others and its sociocultural and biological limitations are precisely acknowledged. And a claim of subjective experience as a source of knowledge that does not at the same time recognize the necessity for *intersubjective* communication and checking is merely a recipe for the nihilism so abhorred by Camus.

Sartre believed that he had created a new and better humanism to replace the rational variety which so many of the intellectuals of his generation had come to hold in contempt. He accused 'passionate moderates' such as Camus, as well as scientifically oriented humanists, of building a 'cult of humanity'.[26] He seemed to think that, in reducing the species to the personal experience of one particular male-type being in one historically isolated epoch, he was making humanist philosophy less arrogant. But it is difficult to see how a rational, moderate and empirical humanist outlook—with its tentative and agnostic approach to knowing, and its recognition of the humble evolutionary origins of human primates—could pose a danger to humankind. It was not liberal skeptics who proclaimed that "man is the being whose project is to be God"[27] or that "there is no universe other than the universe of human subjectivity."[28] In the violent twentieth century which his ideas helped to forge, it was not a belief in the potential for reason in Everyone that made people arrogant; it was a belief in Superman and in his power to create the universe in his own totalitarian image.

Sartre was a master of the tactical maneuver—especially the art of avoiding meaningful debate about his ideas. What if a critic said that there was really nothing in his theory, or that it was absurd? He would answer that awareness of nothingness and absurdity at the very core of all being is recognized by Existentialism as the source of the universal anxiety which the questioner was no doubt feeling at that very moment. What if he were accused of contradicting himself? He would brag about being a *living* contradiction: a bourgeois writer with the lifestyle of an aristocrat who spent his spare time manning the barricades. And he would add that logical contradiction is the necessary engine fuelling the dialectic of history.

What if his writings were considered ambiguous? He would point out that he was merely leaving ample room for readers to exercise the freedom to choose their own meaning. After all, he would say, meaning is a purely subjective matter. "We each create our own reality!" What if certain of his actions were judged to have been hurtful to intimates and harmful to society? The answer was determined by his premises. Existentialism teaches that all action is equally moral; only silence and passivity are not, he would say. All that mattered for Sartre was that the act be an 'authentic' expression of one's being, and that it be chosen in full awareness of the subject's responsibility for the image of humankind being created by that act.

Fair enough! Just as the ideas and literary images expressed by Camus are his legacy to those who come after, so it must be with Jean-Paul Sartre. We are left, in the end, with the view of humanity created by the life 'projects' of these men, and with their aftermath in the lives and ideas of others—especially in the social sciences and humanities and within the humanist movement, where the influence of both thinkers has been powerful and lasting. Perhaps, in this at least, Sartre had it right. We can do no better than to let the long, cold light of posterity be the final judge of the Existential Humanism criticized and agonized over by Albert Camus and propounded with a relish by Jean-Paul Sartre. If the fate of that philosophy is to exemplify an evolutionary dead end in human culture and in humanist thought, then so be it.

NOTES

1 A shorter version of this article was previously published in *Humanist in Canada* (Winter 1999/2000), 22-25; 29.
2 Albert Camus, *The Myth of Sisyphus and Other Essays* (New York, NY: Alfred A. Knopf, 1955/1967), 6.
3 *Ibid.*, 22-3.
4 *Ibid.*, 32.
5 *Ibid.*, 41.
6 Susan Sontag, "Camus' Notebooks" in *Against Interpretation* (New York, NY: Farrar, Straus and Giroux, 1966), 52-60.
7 Albert Camus, *Resistance, Rebellion and Death* (New York, NY: Alfred A. Knopf, 1966/1948), 10.
8 Jean-Paul Sartre, *Sartre by Himself* (New York, NY: Urizen Books, 1977), 19.
9 For a comprehensive examination of the philosophy of Edmund Husserl see Pat Duffy Hutcheon, *Leaving the Cave: Evolutionary Naturalism in Social Scientific Thought* (Waterloo, ON: Wilfrid Laurier University Press, 1996), 217-27.
10 Albert Camus, *Resistance, Rebellion and Death*, 14.
11 Jean-Paul Sartre, *Existentialism and Human Emotions* (New York, NY: The Philosophical Library, 1957), 15.

12 ——————, *Existentialism and Humanism* (London, UK: Methuen, 1948), 29.

13 ——————, *Search for a Method* (New York, NY: Vintage Books, 1963), 177.

14 *Ibid.*, 165.

15 Jean-Paul Sartre, *Existentialism and Human Emotions*, 45.

16 Robert Cummings (Ed.), *The Philosophy of Jean Paul Sartre: Selected Works* (New York, NY: Random House, 1965), 209.

17 *Ibid.*, 427.

18 *Ibid.*

19 Jean-Paul Sartre, *Search for a Method*, 165.

20 Albert Camus, *Resistance, Rebellion and Death*, 91.

21 *Ibid.*, 72.

22 Robert Cummings, *The Philosophy of Jean-Paul Sartre*, 438

23 *Ibid.*, 441.

24 *Ibid.*, 472.

25 Albert Camus, *The Rebel: An Essay on Man* (New York, NY: Vintage Books, 1991/1956), 301.

26 For a modern perspective on passionate moderation see Susan Haack, *Manifesto of a Passionate Moderate: Unfashionable Essays* (Chicago, IL: University of Chicago Press, 1998).

27 Jean-Paul Sartre, *Existentialism and Human Emotions*, 63.

28 *Ibid.*, 50.

14: The Legacy of Isaac Asimov[1]

Asimov was a great humanist who vastly enriched the culture of our time with his entertaining and informative books. Indeed, his influence was so pervasive that much of what he was and believed and valued will live as long as there are people to read and think and wonder. Perhaps most important was his contribution to the struggle against one of the greatest dangers facing humankind in this century: the growth of scientific illiteracy in the population at large, and the resulting cultural dominance of pre-scientific world views.

For Isaac Asimov, it was a matter of grave concern that the scientific approach to knowing was still foreign to the general world culture. He noted that, although science had revolutionized the course of history and opened up the universe for intelligent perusal, it was seldom applied to the social realm and had scarcely dented the world views of most human beings. And he recognized the danger posed by the fact that, conceptually speaking, the majority of Earth's people inhabit a world defined by Bronze Age tribalism. Isaac Asimov decided to devote his life to changing this alarming situation.

The Committed Science Educator

Armed with a uniquely creative imagination, plus a gift for explaining difficult ideas, Asimov assumed a remarkable dual role: that of science-fiction writer and futurist; and that of public educator and interpreter of science. He is most widely celebrated for his science fiction. Not so well known, however, are the goals he sought to achieve through that popular vehicle. He believed that *good* science fiction has two important functions: to warn us about what the future will bring if we continue in our present practices; and to provide young readers with the background of information and the vision of future possibilities necessary for intelligent doubting and scientific creativity.

In his chosen role as educator, Asimov wrote on the subjects of the evolution of human culture in general and of science in particular. He published over 400 titles, including nonfiction essays on scientific and philosophical topics, general history and annotated works on the Bible and other literary classics. He traced the development of Judaism and Christianity by analyzing biblical accounts of human origins and prehistory in the light of what science and historical scholarship have taught us since the Bible was written. He presented the Old Testament as a literary masterpiece, much of it put together around 500 BCE during the period of the Babylonian exile, and representing the collective knowledge and mythology of the most learned members of the Judaic culture. Although he loved and respected the Jewish tradition growing from these roots, he always emphasized that he did not value it above those of other groups. "I just think," he wrote, "that it is more important to be human and to have a human heritage; and I think that it is wrong for anyone to feel that there is anything special about any one heritage of whatever kind. It is delightful for human beings to exist in a thousand varieties... but, as soon as any one variety is thought to be more important than any other, the ground is laid for destroying them all."[2]

Perhaps Asimov's greatest talent as an educator was his ability to articulate for his readers the basic conceptual framework of each of the established disciplines with which he dealt in his books. Like all good teachers, he was well aware that simply transmitting bits of information does not lead to understanding. In addition, he assumed a responsibility for organizing and simplifying new knowledge in astronomy, physics, chemistry, biology and ecology as it became confirmed and established; and for identifying the connections among these studies as well as their implications for the future of humanity. Most of the essays in his various collections are concerned with these matters.

The Significance of Cultural Evolution

As if all that were not enough, Asimov attempted to do the same for history. In his 1991 book, *The March of the Millennia*, he related the evolution of civilization to the development of technology, beginning with the discovery of fire by early hominids. His premise was that it was this crucial technological breakthrough which first distinguished our ancestors from other primates and gave them their evolutionary advantage. As with all subsequent technology, fire made greater demands on primitive communication skills as well as expanding opportunities for their practise. It also increased the food supply of those upright animals who had mastered it and thus made it possible for their range and numbers to increase. As Asimov explained it, from then on natural selection would have ensured that humankind developed the intelligence to become "a tool-designing animal in a large way, and that meant a new kind—and much faster kind—of evolution began to take place."[3]

That new kind of evolution was cultural. It was accelerated considerably by the next great technological revolution, the domestication of plants and animals and the more stable form of social organization that farming required. For Asimov, this signalled the onset of civilization, of "the kind of society that is marked by agriculture and cities."[4] From about 8000 BCE, he said, there was to be no turning back, although the myths of all cultures have expressed a yearning for some dimly remembered Golden Age before the advent of agriculture. Many of these myths reveal, as well, a deeply embedded resentment and scapegoating of women. Asimov related this to the probability that it was the female of the species who initiated seed planting and the caring for animals and, thereby, the more organized, responsible and labour-intensive existence that such practices required.(A further explanation is that it would have been males, freed by a surplus food supply, who had sufficient leisure time to become the first soothsayers and storytellers.)

The arrival of agriculture brought organized warfare in its wake, as successful settlements tried to protect their stores from invaders. Asimov believed this determined the pattern of history for the following twenty centuries. It is the story of an 'evolutionary arms race' (spurred on by population pressures) that generated invention after invention—each providing a temporary resting place for the more innovative civilization. Ultimately, in every case, the 'barbarians without' would co-opt the technology and use it against the settled group.

As examples, Asimov cited the following: the Sumerian invention of the wheel which (along with the taming of wild horses) led eventually to the chariots used by the Kassites to overrun Babylonia; the invention of metallurgy resulting in the iron weapons of the Hittites which were, in turn, used by the Dorians who destroyed the Mycenean and Ionian Greek civilizations; the mounted cavalry and spears and shields usurped by the Assyrian hordes; the technique for telling direction by the stars which enabled the Phoenicians (formerly the settled citizens of Canaan or Palestine) to become the invincible seafaring arm of the early Persian Empire until conquered by the Romans using the same technology; Alexander's successful use of the Theban phalanx and the catapult; the Roman legion formation and the durable roads eventually used by the Goths to destroy the remnants of the empire in its waning days; and so on and on.

Invariably, these technologies were invented by a settled, civilized culture and then used against their originators by successive waves of invaders. Asimov suggested that the tide did not turn in favour of settled civilizations until the introduction of gunpowder in the fifteenth century CE. The tide reversed once more with the discovery of nuclear fission and the revolution in communications and transportation resulting from the other World War II breakthroughs of radar, jet propulsion and the computer. Our crossing of this watershed should sound a warning of the danger posed for dominant cultures by a transfer of the power to wreak untold damage into the hands of the 'barbarians without'. A major theme of all of Asimov's writings is the need for humankind to recognize the significance of these seminal events.

Asimov analyzed all subsequent cultural evolution in terms of technological advance generated by the demands of recurring warfare—sparked, in turn, by population expansion. He claimed that, at every stage of the resulting increase in intellectual and organizational complexity, humanity was faced with only three choices: *abandon, endure,* or *advance.* He further noted that no society has ever voluntarily given up the improvements in quality of life made possible by the current technology. The second option—to *endure*—is simply to be buffeted about as helpless victims of change, with no corresponding social or cultural adaptation. Asimov claimed that the successful societies at every juncture of history have been the ones that chose to *advance.* According to him, this move has always involved attempts to solve, by more appropriate social organization and the invention of ever better technology, the problems of adaptation—including those problems created by previous advances in technology.

This led him to suggest that the concept of world government has been made possible and workable for the first time in history by the very technological innovations that have rendered it imperative. The advent of instantaneous world-wide communication systems and the prospect of open access to the products of global surveillance, along with the technical capability to annihilate all life on Earth, have made the planetary social interdependence we now refer to as 'globalization'[5] a fact of life rather than a distant ideal or threat. From now on, he warned, "The kick you aim at your neighbor will hit your own rear as well."[6] He added that it is time we forgot the myth of 'less than all'—the siren call of tribalism in all its ethnic, religious, and nationalistic forms.

Asimov also warned against what he considered the foolish idea of abandoning technology in our search for solutions, referring to the population explosion as an example of an overriding challenge. As he put it:"Consider mankind's increasing numbers that are outstripping the food supply, outracing the energy resources, outgrowing its room, outraging its ecology."[7] We could, he conceded, forget medical science and allow unbridled plague to decimate our numbers. Or we could accomplish the same end through wholesale famine, by spurning the use of agricultural implements, irrigation, fertilizer—and (one might add) research into the production of seeds with built-in resistance to pests and disease, as well as studies on the genetic sources of human illnesses.

Abandon? He maintained that the organic food trend is not the wave of the future. *Endure?* Or *advance?* He noted wryly that evolution (cultural as well as biological) has only a forward gear. "To go into reverse is sheer unimaginable catastrophe."[8]

The Role of the Computer

Asimov's perspective on the computer was somewhat unique. He wrote that it is the key, not only to a necessarily more complex future, but to the only future that can *work*. He recognized that evolution, whether of biological life or technology, is irreversible and unstoppable. And that, he maintained, means computerization in the broadest possible sense because society has grown too complex to be made to work in any other way. In response to the fear that totalitarianism would be the inevitable political consequence of the comprehensive records (and general accessibility to these) made possible by the computer, he noted that twentieth-century history has shown such systems to have quite the opposite roots and results. In his opinion, complete computerization of society would promote *dissemination* rather than *centralization* of information and power.

Few yet comprehend it fully, but the advent of the computer represented the beginning of the second Industrial Revolution. And even fewer recognize what Asimov considered to be one of the computer's greatest future contributions: its use as an instrument for helping humans determine appropriate solutions to the problems raised by the first Industrial Revolution. "Now perhaps we can plan ways of accomplishing great change while foreseeing with useful clarity the consequences of those changes, and therefore so guiding them as to achieve what we want and expect, rather than stumbling into what we don't want and didn't expect."[9] *What* we want, however, will, then as now, be the result of some sort of collective value judgment, to be realized through a political process which computerization has the potential for rendering increasingly democratic and knowledge-based.

Asimov was convinced that not only will the computer be imperative as a tool for managing democratically determined social change, but it may soon have to operate in the service of another, even more sensitive and profoundly ethical human task. He put it this way: "We have now reached the stage... where the advance of genetic engineering makes it quite conceivable that we will begin to design our own evolutionary progress—and will be stopped from doing so not by any strictly technical difficulty but by the overall ethical problems of deciding how we want to change, what we intend to become, where we want to go."[10] The computer, with its ability to demonstrate the chain of events flowing from every hypothetical option, would be invaluable in preventing grievous irreversible errors here.

The Scientific Approach to Knowing

According to Asimov, there are two attributes absolutely essential to scientific inquiry. The first of these is creativity. He saw nothing essentially mysterious about the phenomenon, whether it be in science or any other field of endeavour. He claimed that creativity merely requires: (1) the possession of as many relevant 'bits' of information as possible; (2) the ability to combine these in a variety of ways with ease and comprehension; (3) the ability to 'intuit', with great rapidity, chains of consequences flowing from new combinations of 'bits'; (4) courage and (5) lots of luck.

The other vital aspect of the scientific orientation is what Asimov called 'a built-in doubter'. One must be able to doubt intelligently; that is, to judge the authoritativeness of the source of a proposition, and the nature of the claim being made for it (the kind of evidence supporting it and the degree that it 'fits' into the current structure of science). If it represents a revolutionary departure, doubt should be very great. He reminded us that even Einstein did not overturn the entire structure of physics. Newton's theory was not proved wrong but merely incomplete, a particular instance of a much broader principle. Asimov claimed that, for the growth of science, doubting is far more important than believing. It is all too easy to be gullible; to doubt requires logic and a depth of knowledge of the field in question. It was his considered opinion that the procedures of scientific inquiry are specifically designed to encourage doubt and prevent easy acceptance of new propositions. This is why experiments must be repeated and observations and measurements confirmed publicly and in a variety of situations by different researchers. It is why speculations that fail to generate hypotheses capable of standing up to such repeated efforts to disprove them fall by the wayside. For Asimov, science was, more than anything, a rigidly formalized procedure for ensuring and satisfying doubt. He pointed out that "all this is nothing more than the setting up of a system of 'natural selection' designed to winnow the fit from the unfit in the realm of ideas, in a manner analogous to the concept of Darwinian evolution. The process may be painful and tedious, as evolution itself is; but in the long run it gets results, as evolution itself does."[11]

Asimov compared science to other disciplines where there is as yet no accepted consensus, describing how the different schools argue endlessly, moving from one fad to another over the centuries. In a field such as sociology, he said, one can be a plausible fake simply by learning the language and speaking with authority. There are no procedures, such as those at the heart of science which, sooner or later, reveal all fraudulent claims. Asimov explained that, because of its internal requirements of testability and replicability, the evidence provided by science is *compelling*. Very few problem areas in the pre-scientific social studies—and *none* of the so called alternative paths to truth—are capable of presenting similarly reliable claims.

Ethical and Ontological Concerns of Humanism

Asimov predicted the end of sexism, in that equality of the sexes has been shown to be associated with the freeing of women from extended responsibility for childbearing. In a world where population expansion means destruction of the biosphere, survival of our species demands that only a relatively few people will raise children. The end of war will come about, he said, not because of any change of heart on the part of the majority but because access for the 'barbarians without' to the tools of mass destruction will mean suicide for the human race unless the world organizes globally to prohibit and contain the use of violence to achieve political ends. Asimov was convinced that the great legal problem of the twenty-first century will be the establishment of a strong world government, combined with regional control wherever global welfare is not at stake.[12] He surmised that the end of racism will necessarily result not only from world government in action but from the need for the people of Earth to cooperate in the collective use, colonization, and protection of space.

The underlying message in all of Asimov's writings is one of thoroughgoing humanism. Not for him were mystical quests for meaning above and apart from the strivings of humanity. In his view, the universe can have meaning "only insofar as its incredible intricacies can be sensed, interpreted, and analyzed by intelligence."[13] He confronted the issue of supernaturally based religious claims in his typically direct fashion, noting that no evidence has been uncovered by science that in any way points to divine guidance in the workings of the universe. Nor is there evidence of the existence of a soul or any other non-natural essence setting humans apart from other animals and departing at death. While admitting that this does not amount to proof that such entities do not exist, he reminded us that the same applies in the case of Zeus, Marduk, Thoth, and a myriad of other supernatural beings. He claimed that "it is not reasonable to demand proof of a negative and to accept the positive in the absence of such proof."[14]

Endurance of the 'Strong Anthropic Principle'

Asimov discussed the tenacity of the 'strong anthropic principle' in human culture: the notion that the universe was formed for the benefit of human beings according to the design of an omnipotent observer. A currently popular revival of this takes the form of an argument (sometimes even presented by accredited scientists) that, because only Earth seems to be conducive to life, these uniquely perfect conditions could not have come about by accident. These people forget that the entire evolutionary process is the ongoing, cumulative result of a series of fortuitous accidents, of which only an infinitesimal few products had what it took to survive. Asimov pointed out that we find our universe perfect because it is the only one that could have brought us to our current form and function.

He explained that the anthropomorphism behind the strong anthropic principle is a remnant of the geocentrism dominating civilized thought from the time of Ptolemy to that of Copernicus and Galileo. He claimed that, even today, most people are geocentric, anthropocentric, ethnocentric, and egocentric. Intellectually they may know better, but emotionally the old infantile self-absorption and tribalism still predominate. The other-world religions, with their myths about authority from on high, cater to these primitive emotions and the fantasies that feed them. Asimov sounded a stark warning concerning the need for a this-world focus. He argued that humanity can no longer afford to seek refuge in the false security of supernatural fantasy, for continued reliance on heavenly solutions could kill us all. Just as it is human beings alone who are destroying the world, he said, so it must be we alone who save it.

The Need for a Scientific Humanism

During the twentieth century, what has been loosely labelled 'humanism' has not always maintained the core of reason and commitment to disciplined inquiry that was its trademark in earlier times. Sometimes the worst enemies of science have been experts in the subjects usually termed the humanities. Asimov reminded us that the humanities have traditionally represented secular learning; that is, the accumulated product of human intelligence. Certain modern scholars in the humanities seem not to have noticed that, since the Renaissance, science has become an overwhelmingly significant aspect of the universal culture. This means that, today, people can no longer claim to be humanists and yet remain ignorant of science for, in so doing, they have deliberately isolated themselves from one of humanity's most important concerns. Similarly, said Asimov, no one can claim to be a humanist in the twenty-first century while refusing to acknowledge the primacy of reason and evidence in the search for knowledge. Concerning this problem, his only source of optimism was the fact that there is al-

ways a new generation coming along with fertile minds as yet un-
encumbered with the rust of age-old myths and prejudices. "We
must present the view of reason," he said, "not in the hope of re-
constructing the desert of ruined minds..., but to educate and train
new and fertile ones."[15]

Perhaps the most compelling argument ever made for a
scientific humanism is contained in Asimov's introduction to his
1978 book, *Life and Time*. He began with Alexander Pope's famous couplet from *An Essay on Man*: "Know then thyself, pre-
sume not God to scan; The proper study of mankind is man." He
then proceeded to analyze the quotation in the context of current
scientific knowledge, identifying the real nature of the antithesis
posed by Pope as being between matters subject to the laws of nature and those assumed to be bound by no laws of any kind. Pope
was presenting humanity's two choices: scientific inquiry leading
to expanding knowledge, or endless speculation leading nowhere.

But what about the emphasis on humanity as the measure
of all things? How are we to answer today's critics of humanism
who claim that the perspective is human-centred to the *exclusion*
of other living things and other aspects of the universe? Asimov
asked, is the study of humans, then, not too confining? His answer
came as a resounding "No!" He explained that such a study is in-
herently and necessarily limitless, for the simple reason that humanity does not exist in a vacuum. Every other form of life affects
or is affected by it; every environmental condition on Earth operates to shape us and is, in turn, altered irrevocably by our activities.
Humankind, like all other forms of life, is a product of the process
of the universe and subject to the same laws.

Furthermore, wrote Asimov, our species is a unique part of
that universe. The human brain is the result of some 15 billion
years of evolution, and we may very well be the only portion of this
vast process with sufficient complexity to be aware of our context
and positioning in space. Indeed, he concluded, if we cannot exist
without the universe, neither can the universe be observed or understood without us. To study humanity *is*, in fact, to study the
universe; and *vice versa*. Surely, then, we should appreciate the
uniqueness and significance of our species in the scheme of things

and revere the evolution that brought us into being! No other known species has developed the creative and powerful instrument of a scientific-inquiry process with the capacity to illuminate the pulse of the universe back to the very beginning and forward to the end of time. Asimov's greatest contribution to humanism may well be his recognition of all this.

NOTES

1 A shorter version of this article was published previously in *The Humanist* (March 1993), 3-5; and republished in *Humanist in Canada* (Spring 2000), 19-20; 38.
2 Isaac Asimov, *In Joy Still Felt: An Autobiography of Isaac Asimov* (New York, NY: Doubleday, 1980), 147.
3 ——————, *Science Past–Science Future* (New York, NY: Doubleday, 1975), 164.
4 ——————, *March of the Millennia* (New York, NY: Walker and Co., 1991), 15.
5 The term 'globalization' is used here in the politically neutral, logical sense of the word, meaning simply the process by which cultural institutions become global in concern and jurisdiction. It applies equally to government, science and technology, the arts, language, education and economic matters.
6 Isaac Asimov, *Life and Time* (New York, NY: Doubleday, 1978), 250.
7 *Ibid.*, 83.
8 *Ibid.*, 84.
9 Isaac Asimov, *The Beginning and the End* (New York, NY: Doubleday, 1977), 172.
10 *Ibid.*, 174.
11 *Ibid.*, 173.
12 Isaac Asimov, *Life and Time*, 251.
13 ——————, *Today, Tomorrow And ...* (New York, NY: Doubleday, 1973), 237.
14 ——————, *In the Beginning* (New York, NY: Crown Publishers, 1981), 11-12.
15 Bette Chambers, "Isaac Asimov: Durable and Enduring Selections." *The Humanist* (Nov./Dec. 1986), 14.

15: Carl Sagan's Scientific Humanism[1]

An appreciation of a man of our times whose life and work personifies the intellectual and ethical approach of modern humanism.

Carl Sagan was one of the greatest humanists who ever lived, although he seldom, if ever, used the term. He devoted his life to educating the public about science—and to educating scientists about their responsibility for how scientific knowledge is used—in an age when both were considered by the academic community to be inappropriate pursuits. He fought a long-term battle against the pseudo-science and anti-science that are spreading like a rot in modern culture. And, through his success in organizing physicists to communicate the message about the nature of the nuclear winter that would predictably result from the deployment of hydrogen bombs, Carl Sagan, more than any other one person, may have been responsible for the avoidance of nuclear war in our lifetime.

Carl was born in 1934, the only son of Jewish immigrants from Russia. His father was a cutter in a New York garment factory. His sister and only sibling says that, as a child "he was always reaching for the stars", and always entranced by the possibility that there might be some form of life elsewhere. His first summer job was in the laboratory of a leading astronomer who was working on the subject of the origin of life on earth. He studied astronomy and astro-physics at the University of Chicago. His PhD dissertation was unique in that it amounted to a significant scientific breakthrough. He had marshalled evidence for the thesis that something had occurred on Venus to produce a devastating Greenhouse Effect, from which the planet had never recovered.

If ever anyone was in the right place at the right time, and with the right credentials, it was Carl Sagan when he graduated in 1957, the year the Russians launched SPUTNIK. He was immediately invited to join the first planetary expedition of the newly formed NASA expedition to Venus (the 1962 Mariner II). He was thus in a position to witness, firsthand, the confirmation of his own doctoral thesis. This established his reputation as a major scientist at the very moment in history when U. S. space research was being launched.

In 1963 Sagan was hired by Harvard to teach astronomy. While there he was involved with Mariner IV, NASA's first probe to Mars. The news of an environment apparently hostile to life was a crushing disappointment to him. At the same time, he was finding himself increasingly lonely at Harvard, and Harvard was becoming increasingly unhappy with him. They were not comfortable with an astronomer and physicist who wanted to educate the ordinary person about science; and to educate scientists about their unique responsibility for the future of life and human culture. In 1968 he was passed over for tenure. While this is usually the kiss of death for a young academic, Sagan was immediately snapped up by Cornell University. He became the Director of their new Laboratory for Planetary Sciences, and remained in that capacity until his death in December of 1996.

Meanwhile, in 1969, when NASA put Apollo II on the moon, Sagan was one of the experts responsible for briefing the astronauts. One of the subsequent 'pioneer missions' to space carried a Galactic Greeting which he had designed. He was by then campaigning for another mission to Mars—one that would actually land there. Viking II was sent in 1976. It became the first manmade object to send pictures of the Martian landscape back to earth. The pictures revealed a surprisingly familiar-looking rocky desert with no evidence of life.

In 1977 Carl Sagan became a media star with the publication of his popular book, *The Dragons of Eden*. That same year he and Ann Druyan, who was to become his third wife, produced a disk to be taken into space. It was called *Sounds of Planet Earth*. Sagan referred to it as "a message in a bottle thrown into the future." Also that same year, he and Ann began planning a thirteen-part television series titled *Cosmos*: a project that lasted three years and required filming in twelve different countries. It was aired in 1980, the same year The Voyager spacecraft sent back the first pictures ever taken of Jupiter and Saturn. In 1981 the launch of the shuttle Columbia marked the end of NASA's program of large-scale space travel. In 1982 the American Congress allocated funds to support a long-sought official search for extra-terrestrial intelligence. During this period Sagan suffered a severe, life-threatening illness. For these, and a number of additional reasons, he began to focus all of his remarkable talents and energies on the prospects for continuing life here on our apparently unique and fragile Earth.

Near the end of his life Sagan told of being asked by a student: "Now that you have successfully debunked everything that we have been taught to believe about the human role and origin in the Universe, what is there left for us?" His answer for the student, and for all human beings, was to "do something worthwhile with this amazing life while you have it!"

Did Carl Sagan in fact merely tear down old beliefs without putting anything better in their place? Even for those who never met him, he left behind a treasure trove of published works which put the lie to that accusation. His life was dedicated, not to tearing down, but to building a positive, integrated world view capable of providing better guidance for human beings in the centuries to come than our ancient inherited mythologies could ever do.

Sagan was worried about the welfare of a humankind that was being forced to navigate the perilous waters of the future with one foot aboard the seaworthy craft of science and the other embedded in the quicksand of mysticism along the shore. "We compartmentalize," he said, referring even to the highly schooled among us. "Some scientists do this too, effortlessly stepping between the skeptical world of science and the credulous world of religious belief without missing a beat... But we cannot have science in bits and pieces, applying it where we feel safe and ignoring it where we feel threatened."[2] He explained that science is a way of thinking much more than it is a body of knowledge. It provides an integrated, yet evolving and open-ended, frame of reference for making sense out of experience—all experience. The goal of science is to discover how the world works, to look for regularities, to understand the connections of things. It is an all-encompassing approach, rooted in childhood trial-and-error forays into our surroundings and the learnings resulting from the consequences of such everyday 'experiments' in living. And it develops from there, with no discrete break, into the formal public endeavour requiring open and precise communication of research plans and methods as well as a collective process of checking up on results.

Sagan admitted that the results of scientific inquiry can never be the 'Truths' or 'essence of reality' claimed by mystics and purportedly embodied in the mythologies of most religions. This means that they cannot offer us the illusion of certainty that so many religious natures seem to crave. But they are by far the best that fallible humans can ever hope for. Sagan quoted Einstein's famous comment that, "all of our science, measured against reality, is primitive and childlike—and yet it is the most precious thing we have."[3] He warned that there are already many signs that American culture may be on the verge of forsaking science for mysticism, and thereby sliding back almost without noticing it into superstition and the darkness that engulfed our demon-haunted world for thirteen centuries after the fall of Rome.

Sagan explained that, at the heart of science, there are two distinguishing features making it uniquely valuable as the foundation of a workable world view. One of these is the self-correcting mechanism which not only allows for, but encourages, an unrelenting process of testing propositions in terms of their workability and falsifiability. The other is an essential balance between two attitudes: "an openness to new ideas, no matter how counter-intuitive, and the most ruthlessly skeptical scrutiny of all ideas, old and new."[4]

Sagan had good reason to be concerned about the attacks that have been mounted against science in recent years. Many of these have come from the literary and philosophical movement referred to loosely as 'postmodernism'. Proponents of the scientific world view have been accused by the postmodernists of 'idolizing' science; and of belonging to a secret, elite society seeking to maintain a monopoly on specialized knowledge which is no different in its essence from the truth claims of New Age mysticism. It has even been claimed that scientists are arrogant power mongers who negotiate and/or impose their theories upon the rest of us; that they are as prejudiced as anyone else; and that throughout history their theories have been merely reflections of their own class and gender biases with no more dependability than 'any other form of ideology'. As a group, scientists have been called 'nerdy left-brainers', arrogant destroyers of the awe and wonder of nature, and architects of the 'disenchantment' of humanity. They are said to be obsessed with imposing an artificial order on nature for the satisfaction of their own needs when, in fact, the new physics has demonstrated that reality is random and chaotic and, in its very essence, 'unknowable'.

Unlike most scientists who prefer to remain above the fray, Sagan felt that he had a responsibility to the future to respond to such charges. As to the first of the above, he said, the scientific method of inquiry is "far from being idolatry. [It is, instead,] the means by which we can distinguish the false idols from the real thing."[5] And as for science being secretive, Sagan maintained that it is the most publicly communicated and objectively tested endeavour in all of human culture. In response to the common criticism that quantum mechanics is no less mysterious than shamanistic or theological or New Age beliefs, he said that, even if we cannot understand it, we can verify that quantum mechanics works. In fact, we don't have to understand a scientific theory fully in order to observe what it predicts. It is the *unreliability* of the predictions of mystical doctrines that marks them as useless.

Sagan explained as well that "scientists do not seek to impose their needs and wants on Nature, but instead humbly interrogate Nature and take seriously what they find."[6] In fact scientific theories, by their very nature, cannot be negotiated or politically imposed. The process of interrogating Nature is necessarily a two-way enterprise, with Nature fighting back in no uncertain terms if the questioner gets out of line. Theories from which refutable hypotheses cannot be derived are simply not scientific. Those implying testable propositions that are subsequently refuted are discarded. It is this periodic discarding of disconfirmed and unfruitful theories which is the source of those very revolutions in science that so many people fail to understand. The 'facts' or regularities revealed by scientific inquiry have not altered—only the theory explaining and guiding the process has been replaced, with the older one remaining in use in those circumstances where it continues to 'work'. Sagan concluded that it may well be this rapid rate of change in science in recent times which is responsible for some of the fire it draws, and for the accusation that it is merely one among a number of competing ideologies.

Many social scientists are guilty of pandering to anti-science thinking, according to Sagan. They want to have it both ways: to have the respect traditionally granted to science in the public domain without being burdened by its methods and rules. They seem not to understand, he said, that the credibility of science is a consequence of its *method*—the very thing that they either fail to comprehend or stubbornly refuse to follow. And their deficient methodologies and fallacious theories multiply, he said, for bad science inevitably drives out good. He also deplored the way popular tabloids contribute to a confusion of pseudo-science with science by their concerted attempt to make science (the very instrument of skeptical inquiry) appear to confirm ancient faiths and popular occult propositions—all of which are devised in such a way that they are neither subject to disconfirmation nor amenable to rational discussion. The latter are limbic, right-hemisphere-inspired doctrines, Sagan explained. Although natural human responses to the complexity of our surroundings, they are fatally limited if not subjected to the intervention of the fully functioning neocortex, with its left-hemispheric reason working through the world's inputs as they are actually experienced.

The charge that scientists are no more objective than anyone else—and fully as prone to pursuing their own self-interests—has nothing to do with the reliability of science in general, according to Sagan. It is the foregoing institutionalized inquiry method that distinguishes science from pseudo-science, not the value neutrality of its practitioners. Science thrives on errors, he said, correcting or discarding them one by one. Pseudo-science does the opposite, framing propositions precisely so that they are *invulnerable* to falsifiability. Incredibly, the onus is then placed on doubters to disprove them! However, Sagan recognized that the relative success of pseudo-science today rests upon something else as well—on an alarming upsurge of credulity within the population. "Our politics, advertising and religions (New Age and Old) are awash in credulity. Those who have something to sell, those who wish to influence public opinion, those in power, a skeptic might suggest, have a vested interest in discouraging skepticism."[7] Without scientific habits of thought, he said, "we risk becoming a... world of suckers, up for grabs by the next charlatan who saunters along. [Precious television time is devoted to teaching our children] murder, rape, cruelty, superstition, credulity and consumerism... What kind of society could we create if, instead, we drummed into them science and a sense of hope?"[8]

As for the popular claim that science destroys our sense of wonder and has contributed to the 'disenchantment' of humanity, Sagan would have none of it. He reminded us that any protozoology or bacteriology textbook is filled with wonders that far outshine those derived from the hallucinatory imaginings of mystics and pseudo-scientists. And why, he asked, is a sense of enchantment founded on ignorance considered more desirable than the self-knowledge available through authentic science? "If we long to believe that the stars rise and set for us, that we are the reason there is a Universe, does science do us a disservice by deflating our conceits?"[9]

Sagan also pointed out numerous times that "the order of the Universe is not an assumption; it is an observed fact."[10] And that the simplest definition of science is the search for rules—which is, in turn, the only possible way to understand our vast and complex Universe. He noted that "human beings are, understandably, highly motivated to find regularities, natural laws... The Universe forces those who live in it to understand it. Those creatures who find everyday experience a muddled jumble of events with no predictability, no regularity, are in grave peril. The Universe belongs to those who, at least to some degree, have figured it out."[11] As for it being 'unknowable', he commented as follows:

> For myself, I like a Universe that includes much that is unknown and, at the same time, much that is knowable. A universe in which everything is known would be static and dull, as boring as the heaven of some weak-minded theologians. A Universe that is unknowable is no fit place for thinking beings. The ideal Universe for us is very much like the one we inhabit. And I guess that is really not much of a coincidence.[12]

More than anything, Sagan feared the consequences of scientific illiteracy in the public at large. "When governments and societies lose the capacity for critical thinking, the results can be catastrophic—however sympathetic we may be for those who have bought the baloney."[13] Elsewhere he quoted an egregious example of what can happen when elite opinion shapers connive to encourage general gullibility. "A new era of the magical explanation of the world is rising, an explanation based on will rather than knowledge. There is no truth in either the moral or the scientific sense."[14] The speaker of these words was Adolf Hitler, but the sentiments had been encouraged by the intellectual ancestors of today's 'postmodernist' philosophers for at least a century.

Humanists will be interested in what Carl Sagan had to say about religion. In one of his earliest books he spelled out the basis of his scientific agnosticism, as applied to religious belief. "Those who raise questions about the God hypothesis and the soul hypothesis are by no means all atheists. An atheist is someone who is certain that God does not exist, someone who has compelling evidence against the existence of God. I know of no such compelling evidence... Considering the enormous emotional energies with which the subject is invested, a questing, courageous and open mind seems to be essential for narrowing our collective ignorance on the subject."[15] He had little respect for anyone who held to dogmatic claims of any kind about the ultimate nature of reality. "The idea that scientists or theologians, with our present and still puny understanding of this vast and awesome cosmos, can comprehend the origin of the universe is only a little less silly than the idea that the Mesopotamian astronomers of 3000 years ago—from whom the ancient Hebrews borrowed, during the Babylonian captivity, the cosmological accounts in the first chapter of Genesis—could have understood the origins of the universe."[16]

Sagan did not attack traditional religions, but he did chide them for having made a fatal mistake in continuing to assert truth claims about the nature of the cosmos and about the origins and destiny of humankind: claims that are the business of science. He thought that religion could make a positive contribution to modern society only if it forsook myth and mysticism and concentrated on activities having to do with reverence for life, awe at the wonders of nature, ethics and morality, community, the celebration of life's passages and striving for social justice.

Sagan distinguished clearly between mysticism and spirituality. While mysticism is concerned with matters of magic, the occult, spiritualism, the supersensual and 'essentially unknowable', the human spirit is something quite different. "It comes from the Latin word 'to breathe'," he wrote. "What we breathe is air, which is certainly matter, however thin. Despite usage to the contrary, there is no necessary implication in the word 'spirituality' that we are talking about anything other than matter (including the realm of matter of which the brain is made) or anything outside the realm of science... Science is not only compatible with spirituality; it is a profound source of spirituality... The notion that science and spirituality are somehow mutually exclusive does a profound disservice to both."[17] Carl Sagan was never unkind or arrogant when referring to religious believers. He was all too aware of the fallibility of all of us, and of the human need for fellowship and for reassurance and wish-fulfilment in a frighteningly complex world. Rather than blaming or deriding the victims, he cited the culture in which most people are being socialized: a culture in which the tools of skepticism are not generally being made available to children. He thought that the present situation is fraught with peril for the human race. In the end, his final message was that it is only the candles lit by the scientific method that stand between us and the gathering darkness.

NOTES

1 Previously published in *Humanist in Canada* (Autumn 1997), 6-9; 33.
2 Carl Sagan, *The Demon-Haunted World: Science as a Candle in the Dark* (New York, NY: Random House, 1996), 297.
3 *Ibid.*, 2.
4 *Ibid.*, 304.
5 *Ibid.*, 31.
6 *Ibid.*, 32.
7 *Ibid.*, 77.
8 *Ibid.*, 39.
9 *Ibid.*, 12.
10 *Ibid.*, 273.
11 Carl Sagan, *Broca's Brian: Reflections on the Romance of Science* (New York, NY: Random House, 1974), 16.
12 *Ibid.*, 18.
13 Carl Sagan, *The Demon-Haunted World: Science as a Candle in the Dark*, 209.
14 *Ibid.*, 261.
15 Carl Sagan, *Broca's Brain: Reflections on the Romance of Science*, 236.
16 *Ibid.*, 287.
17 Carl Sagan, *The Demon-Haunted World: Science as a Candle in the Dark*, 29-30.

16: The Humanism of Edward O. Wilson[1]

A prominent zoologist outlines the framework of a comprehensive new paradigm for the life and social sciences. This evolutionary-systems perspective is based on reliable findings in evolution studies, human genetics, cognitive- and neuropsychology and Wilson's own revolutionary contribution to inter-disciplinary scholarship: the new field of 'sociobiology'.

A few late-twentieth-century anthropologists and biologists have been leading the way toward the establishment of a scientifically sound, evolutionarily based conceptual framework for the social-psychological sciences. The particular relevance of this for humanism is that the theoretical model which prevails in social science will necessarily provide the foundation for modern humanist philosophy as well. The reason is obvious. The humanist world view is, above all, about what it means to be human. It concerns the origins, potential and power of, and the ethical options for, humanity in the current age. It is difficult to develop a viable humanism in the absence of reliable knowledge about these matters. Unfortunately, much of what has been communicated as social 'science' up to now has, in fact, tended more toward ideology than science. In general, humanists have done well to disregard it in fashioning their world view. As we discovered in the past, any humanism depending on nothing sounder than popular ideologies for its definitions and understandings of the human species is built upon shaky foundations indeed.

Because of the proto-scientific nature of most of the social

studies throughout their short history (coupled with a universal reluctance to accept the significance of the theory of evolution for
human behaviour), the only authentic *scientific* model for humanists to look to until recent times was assumed to be the one organizing and informing the study of physics and astronomy. From
Aristotle to our Enlightenment forebears to the rationalists and
Existentialists of twentieth-century humanism, the imperative either to imitate or reject the logic of the physical sciences has sometimes led humanist thought into strange pathways.

As we enter the third millennium, however, the situation has
grown more promising. We now have access to a comprehensive
candidate for paradigm status in science: one which combines the
new systems theory from physics and the latest findings of neurological science with a greatly increased understanding of the process
of cultural as well as organic evolution. This means we have available
to us, for the first time ever, a model with the potential for applica-
bility to all levels of existence. These revolutionary developments in
the philosophy of science could be said to represent the wave of the
future for humanism. Any humanist philosophy that fails to take account of them is likely to be condemned to irrelevance.

Gene-Culture Co-evolution

Although Edward O. Wilson is an outstanding original contributor to the building of this new integrated evolutionary-systems
perspective, he would be the first to point out that he is not the
only one. In 1964, the year Wilson and his student Stuart Altman
came up with the term 'sociobiology', a two-part article by the
British biologist William Hamilton was published in the *Journal of
Theoretical Biology*. It was called "The Genetic Evolution of Social
Behaviour." As Wilson notes in his autobiography, this article was
to become the keystone of the new inter-disciplinary study. It offered a compelling explanation of how self-sacrifice and cooperation can become genetically fixed traits: an explanation that has
stood the test of subsequent scientific research. Wilson says that he
underwent a 'paradigm shift' after reading and re-reading that article and relating its conclusions to his own findings.

Another early contributor to the new model is Robin Fox, founder of the anthropology department at Rutgers University and, currently, University Professor of Social Theory at that institution. Fox began in the late 1960s to write papers and books critical of the prevailing anti-biological stance of the social sciences. His 1971 book *The Imperial Animal* (co-authored by Lionel Tiger) signalled a radical departure from the reigning ideologies in his field, and gained both writers considerable notoriety. Subsequent works by Fox contributed further to the development of a new co-evolutionary model for a still-generally unreceptive social science. Among these were the 1975 *Biosocial Anthropology* (which he edited) and his subsequent books, including *The Red Lamp of Incest: An Inquiry Into the Origins of Mind and Society* (1983); *The Search for Society: Quest for a Biosocial Science and Morality* (1989) and *Conjectures and Confrontations* (1997).

Until recently, neither scholar has been widely recognized for his contributions to modern humanism. One reason for this is the bad press with which any biological approach to social science has invariably been greeted. Wilson's 1975 book, *Sociobiology: The New Synthesis*, was even less well received by the academic community than was *The Imperial Animal*. Indeed, the virulent and abusive criticism it garnered was equalled only by that directed at B. F. Skinner in previous decades and at Darwin almost a century before. And no wonder! All these thinkers were suggesting the unthinkable. Their message was that even the most complex of the mental aspects of the human species, those which had been attributed previously to some mysterious transcendental force, could be explained by something as simple and natural as the process of natural selection.[2] In fact, when Skinner dared to apply this principle specifically to human behaviour (by recognizing the 'selective' function of the reinforcement of certain behaviours and beliefs as a result of their consequences in determining the individual's impact on the surroundings) he was accused of denying the very existence of the 'inner man'. Wilson, in his turn, was said to be *reducing* human beings to their genes and proposing the return to a long-discredited, ruthless genetic determinism.

In both cases the facts were very different, as anyone willing to read the writings concerned would have learned. Although Skinner referred to himself as a humanist, it seemed that few even of those who shared his world view were willing to give him the benefit of the doubt sufficiently to study his work. For a long time it was the same in the case of Wilson. His ideas were misrepresented and even caricatured by many in the humanist community—particularly in Europe. There and elsewhere, people who identified themselves chiefly in terms of politics were all too ready to accuse Wilson of dire political purposes. However, as has been amply demonstrated, such charges were quite unwarranted.[3] Wilson (with his co-writer, Lumsden) was careful to define the proposed new study as "neither a particular theory of behavior nor... a politically defined doctrine of human nature. [Rather, it is]... a systematic study of the biological basis of all forms of social behavior... in organisms up to and including man."[4]

The proposed evolutionary perspective was explained as follows:

> We believe the secret of the mind's sudden emergence lies in the activation of a mechanism both obedient to physical laws and unique to the human species. Somehow the evolving species kindled a Promethean fire, a self-sustaining reaction that carried humanity beyond the previous limits of biology. This largely unknown evolutionary process we have called gene-culture coevolution: it is a complicated, fascinating interaction in which culture is generated and shaped by biological imperatives while biological traits are simultaneously altered by genetic evolution in response to cultural innovation.[5]

If Wilson had provided us with nothing else, humanists should be forever grateful for the concept of 'gene-culture coevolution'. Although not original with him, it is spelled out in his writings in terms understandable to the general reader. The concept opens the door to a new understanding of the key role of evolution—not only in the biological history of the species, but in the culture of humanity. At the same time, it emphasizes the complexity of the interaction between the two. It promises to provide a sound, scientific and philosophical foundation for any humanist world view that takes evolution into account. However, Wilson's contributions did not stop there. His works on the nature of human nature present a human being abundantly in accord with the best of humanist thought throughout the ages: one rich in thinking, feeling and valuing potential, but totally forged out of the natural process of biological and cultural co-evolution. And he offers a definitive criterion and evolutionary source for the origin of culture in the instinctive capacity for language that both social scientists and humanists would do well to note. Evolution has produced a symbolic coding deep within the human brain, he says, which functions to allow us to build internal representations of the world. This language instinct "consists of precise mimicry, compulsive loquacity, near-automatic mastery of syntax, and the precise acquisition of a large vocabulary. The instinct is a diagnostic and evidently unique human trait, based upon a mental power beyond the reach of any [other] animal species, and it is the precondition of true culture."[6]

Wilson explains that it is this advanced capacity for language which has made the human species both uniquely vulnerable to, and able to benefit from, that particular form of socialization known as *enculturation*. The latter can be interpreted specifically as the acquisition of ideas, customs, and ideals from the culture—what political scientists sometimes equate with 'indoctrination'. According to Wilson, *socialization* (interpreted as the more general process of learning from environmental demands and opportunities) is common to all animals, but the language-based openness to learning which has evolved in humans has an added dimension. He says it makes them absurdly easy to indoctrinate. In fact, he adds, "They *seek* it."[7] And, given the depths of superstition and hatred and the heights of knowledge and human understanding obtainable thereby, that vulnerability to indoctrination has made all the difference![8]

In other animals, socialization tends to be restricted to the learning of species-characteristic behaviour, passed along from generation to generation by means of modelling and imitation. An example is the behaviour of prairie dogs in building towns capable of providing protection from predators as well as encouraging the growth of the plants on which they feed. It is also exemplified in the recent finding that baby elephants raised in captivity, in isolation from mature members of their species, acquire none of the behaviours necessary for raising their young. The complex communication systems found among bees, varying from hive to hive, are also learned capacities that co-evolve along with their genetic endowments.[9]

Wilson has even offered a co-evolutionary explanation for the sensation of 'free will'. While reminding us that any real comprehension of human decision making must await further progress in neurobiology, he presents the following tentative hypothesis:

> An organism can be guided in its actions by a feedback loop: a sequence of messages from the sense organs to the brain schemata back to the sense organs and on around again until the schemata 'satisfy' themselves that the correct action has been completed. The mind could be a republic of such schemata, programmed to compete among themselves for control of the decision centers, individually waxing and waning in power in response to the relative urgency of the physiological needs of the body being signaled to the conscious mind, then the brain stem and midbrain. 'Will' might be the outcome of the competition, requiring the action of neither a 'little man' nor any external agent.[10]

Kin Selection

Also of significance to humanism is Wilson's clarification and expansion of William Hamilton's previously little-known theory of 'kin selection'. Wilson recounts in his autobiography, *Naturalist*,[11] how he had initially become interested in the issues explained by Hamilton when he read Julian Huxley's 1932 book, *Problems of Relative Growth*. That interest was furthered as the result of a discussion with Huxley at Harvard in 1954 on the subject of population biology. The concept of 'kin selection' led, in turn, to some of Wilson's most salient insights concerning the evolutionary origins of altruism.

He explains that there are two kinds of altruism: 'hard-wired' or genetically determined, and the 'soft-wired' or reciprocal variety which is environmentally programmed (although built upon innate propensities). The former is explained by the phenomenon of kin selection, manifested not only in pair bonding and parent-child bonding, but in the self-sacrificing behaviour of siblings, whose genes are carried on by the children of the brothers and sisters whom they protect—even though they do not them-selves reproduce. According to Wilson, "This form of natural se-lection... can cause a spread of altruistic behavior toward close kin other than offspring... In human beings and a few of the most in-telligent monkeys and apes, the circle of altruism is broadened by reciprocal altruism. In this soft-core form of giving, the act is per-formed with the expectation that the beneficiary will repay in kind at some future date."[12]

Wilson notes the irony involved in the fact that it is this lat-ter, 'self-serving' form of altruism which is badly needed in today's world, while the genetically transmitted 'unselfish' form is at the root of the tribalism now posing such a threat to the future of all life on earth. However, he holds out some hope by reminding us that "the form and intensity of altruistic acts are to a large extent culturally determined. Human social evolution is obviously more cultural than genetic. The point is that the underlying emotion, powerfully manifested in virtually all human societies, is what is considered to evolve through the genes."[13]

In this connection, he also offers an enlightening conjec-ture concerning two sources of a possible genetic basis for homo-sexuality. One is that homosexual genes may confer superior fitness in the heterozygous condition. "The simplest way genes producing such a condition can be maintained in evolution is if they are supe-rior in the heterozygous state, that is, if heterozygotes survive into maturity better, produce more offspring, or both."[14] The second hypothesis is based on the theory of kin selection. Wilson notes that homosexuals in primitive societies may have functioned as helpers, assisting their close relatives. He suggests the strong possibility of homosexuality being normal in the biological sense, "a distinctive beneficial behavior that evolved as an important element in human social organization. Homosexuals may be the genetic carriers of some of mankind's rare altruistic impulses."[15]

The Need For Consilience

A careful reading of Wilson's works on bio-diversity could help us build a new ethic for the third millennium: one focusing on the need to reduce the devastating size of our ecological footprint on planet Earth, while avoiding the anti-science excesses of some environmental activists.[16] His recent book, *Consilience,* discusses the subject in depth. This book deserves special attention for a number of reasons, not the least of which because it appears to be a rather complete formulation of Wilson's own humanist world view. It would seem to be required reading not only for those who aspire to humanism, but for all who recognize the need to consider our problems and concerns in empirical and interdisciplinary terms. The book expresses what is obviously an integration of ideas from Wilson's own life's work in biology, along with conclusions derived from a broad background of reading in the history and philosophy of science. It is, as the title promises, about "consilience, literally a 'jumping together' of knowledge by the linking of facts and fact-based theory across disciplines to create a common ground of explanation."[17] His argument that the search for unifying rules and concepts is the wave of the future is shown throughout to be well-warranted both in terms of past and present successes in the physical sciences (which have tended to focus on problem areas that cross academic disciplines), and the corresponding *failure* of the social sciences and humanities (which have been handicapped by mutually incompatible models tied to traditional disciplinary boundaries).

Clearly Wilson did not intend this book only for humanists and interdisciplinary academics who are already convinced of the need to accept the scientific endeavour in all scholarly pursuits: those whom he terms the modern empiricists. Rather, he attempts to reach the more unsatisfied and questioning of the thoughtful searchers still trapped in the older, anti-science transcendental mythologies that would appear to demand a rigid separation of humanity from the rest of nature—potential humanists, in other words. He does this by following Einstein in expanding the concept of 'being religious' to include the sense of wonder and awe involved in empirical inquiry into the workings of the natural universe. In Wilson's terms, the religious quest is thus broadened to cover the general human desire for meaning and understanding, and for control of one's surroundings—what many people would call our natural human spiritual yearnings.

He calls the preference for a search for objective reality over revelation a Stoic's creed, another way of satisfying what has been experienced in the past as religious hunger. The difference is that this empirical creed aims to salve the spirit not by surrender, but by liberation of the human mind. And the greatest enterprise of that mind in every age, he tells us, has been the attempted linkage of the sciences and humanities in a world view capable of making sense of both as creative human enterprises. According to Wilson, we don't have to live with fractured bits of unrelated findings. "The ongoing fragmentation of knowledge and resulting chaos in philosophy are not reflections of the real world, but artifacts of scholarship."[18] Elsewhere he notes that much of the current mess in philosophy may be due to the fact that the Enlightenment was actually dead for that enterprise by the early nineteenth century, with its ideal of open inquiry into the order of the universe continuing to live on solely as a spur to the *physical* sciences.

Humanists will especially appreciate the reference to Francis Bacon's 'idols of the mind'. These are: (1) *the idols of the tribe* (a false myth-based order imposed upon their experience by humans—which they then use to imprison themselves within a cave of their own creation); (2) *the idols of the marketplace* ('reification' or belief in the reality of an abstraction merely because someone has devised a word to symbolize it); and (3) *the idols of the theatre* (the tendency to accept without question the pronouncements of artfully articulate, influential authority figures). Wilson offers, as examples, various cultural currents that have threatened scientific progress since the Enlightenment, from the recurring waves of Romanticism to the present dominance of the postmodernists. He describes the latter as "a rebel crew milling beneath the black flag of anarchy"[19]; but argues that they, like their similarly reactionary predecessors, may serve indirectly to strengthen science. He suggests that the external enemy creates pressures for us to sharpen our arguments, better explain our theories and more definitively to corroborate our findings—all of which might contribute to general scientific progress in the long run.

Wilson claims that the greatest schism in the world today is the divide between pre-scientific and scientific cultures; for the former must inevitably remain without the means of adapting to changing circumstance, and are thus necessarily regressive. He reminds us that no method of inquiring into the nature of reality other than the empirical one has ever worked: "no exercise from myth, revelation, art, trance or any other conceivable means; and *notwithstanding the emotional satisfaction it brings,* mysticism, the strongest pre-scientific probe into the unknown, has yielded zero."[20] [Emphasis added.]

He goes on to suggest that the greatest challenge facing science today is the accurate and complete description of complex systems. He explains that the much-misunderstood chaos theory simply states that "extremely complicated, outwardly indecipherable patterns can be determined by small, measurable changes within the system."[21] This has the economy and simplicity of all potentially powerful theories, but he emphasizes that the pressing need is for supporting empirical data. A related challenge is to understand more thoroughly the operation and products of the human brain, and how it relates to culture and its evolution. As one would expect, Wilson thinks that a combination of complexity theory and the evolutionary approach is the way to go in neuroscience. "Brain scientists have vindicated the evolutionary view of mind... [by establishing] that passion is inseverably linked to reason. Emotion is not a perturbation of reason but a vital part of it."[22]

As previously noted, Wilson's elaborations of 'gene-culture coevolution' are of particular value to modern humanism. His thesis is that "the human being has evolved genetically by *natural selection in behavior,* just as it has in the anatomy and physiology of the brain."[23] He hypothesizes that, to genetic evolution, "natural selection has added the parallel track of cultural evolution, and the two forms of evolution are somehow linked."[24] According to Wilson, although many animal species manifest complex social behaviours and routines, *culture* is unique to humans. This is because of the language instinct which our species happened to evolve. He explains that what is genetically inherited is not the 'memes' (Richard Dawkins' term for those basic ideas or symbolic units comprising any culture) but the underlying *propensity* to invent and transmit certain kinds of these elements of memory in preference to others. In other words, we inherit a bias to learn in certain directions. Biological and cultural evolution are thus interrelated and interactive, and Wilson suggests that one cannot be studied effectively in isolation from the other.

In the above task, he is not counting on much help from sociology and anthropology—other than in the provision of examples of what *not* to do. In this rather harsh judgment it may appear that he fails to give evolutionary anthropologists such as Robin Fox their due. However, Fox might well agree with him. He recognizes that his field is still dominated by the 'cultural' rather than the evolutionary-systems model; and he concludes that "cultural anthropology, with its rampant doctrine of cultural relativism, is in fact a bastard child of German romantic nationalism."[25]

Wilson thinks that hope for the future lies in the fact that we already have four tentative bridges across the gaping divide between the two fields of study. These are: (1) cognitive neuroscience; (2) human behavioural genetics; (3) evolutionary biology—including his own discipline of sociobiology; and (4) environmental science. In addition, he notes that there is one enterprise within the social sciences which most resembles the physical sciences in style, and is accordingly best posed to bridge the gap between the two. It is economics. However, that study is limited by the same problems shared by population genetics and environmental science.

> It is battered by 'exogenous shocks', all the unaccountable events of history and environmental change that push the parameter values up and down... Except in the most general and statistical terms, economic models cannot forecast the onset of bull and bear markets, or the decades-long cycles triggered by war and technological innovation. They cannot tell us whether tax cuts or deficit reduction is the more effective in raising per capita income, or how economic growth will affect income distribution."[26]

A second fundamental difficulty with economics, according to Wilson, is that it lacks a solid foundation of knowledge in the area of neuropsychology. He notes that the seldom-acknowledged premises of most of those building models in economics are

based on nothing more reliable than 'folk psychology'. Consequently, the enterprise is badly crippled by a lack of understanding
of the function of *incentives* as they actually operate in determining individual behaviours in real-life settings. He points to the
dominant 'rational choice' model in economics as a good example
of this weakness.

Wilson devotes a chapter of *Consilience* to ethics and religion. He presents the intriguing thesis that "the choice between
transcendentalism and empiricism will be the coming century's
version of the struggle for men's souls. Moral reasoning will either
remain centered in idioms of theology and philosophy... or it will
shift toward science-based material analysis."[27] He acknowledges
the power of our deeply entrenched biases toward ancient
mythologies of the supernatural, even admitting to his own personal yen for the comforts of deism. However, for Wilson, this is
accompanied by a recognition of the impossibility of either confirming or refuting the hypothesis of a non-interfering creative
force, along with a bias toward the idea of a strictly *naturalistic*
source of ethics. He presents a fascinating debate between a transcendentalist and empiricist, showing himself to be firmly in the
empirical camp. He then concludes that the eventual result of the
struggle between the two world views will be "the secularization
of the human epic and of religion itself."[28] (The supreme triumph
of humanism?)

Following this introduction Wilson discusses the fact that,
in the future, hereditary change will depend less upon natural selection than upon social choice. Understandably, he becomes
something of a prophet in this concluding section of the book,
pointing out the horrendous environmental consequences of our
continued refusal to attack the problems we have created by our
failure to build reliable unifying systems of knowledge. He sums
up the arguments for the likelihood of catastrophe as follows: (1)
Homo sapiens is approaching the limits of its food and water supply; (2) most of the stress on the environment originates with a
handful of industrialized countries; and (3) even if the industrial-
ization of the developing countries were only partially successful,
the resulting population explosion and environmental aftershock

would dwarf anything we can possibly imagine—and it may well be irreversible. He adds that it would be a mathematical impossibility for the living standards of inhabitants of the third world even to begin to approach those of the industrialized countries. We simply cannot extend to all the world's peoples our unwarranted and dangerous privilege to pollute with ever more people and their products. We must, instead, remove that privilege here at home, and lower expectations everywhere. Otherwise, he says, Rwanda is the microcosm of the world of the future.

Consilience drives home the worrying recognition that humankind has created massive problems for which solutions are neither easy nor obvious. Nevertheless, humanists who, like Wilson, are sometimes understandably pessimistic about the future can take comfort from his stirring admonition that "the moral imperative of humanism is the endeavor alone, whether successful or not, provided the effort is honorable and the failure memorable." [29]

NOTES

1 Sections of this essay were previously published in "Fear Ignorance, Not Sociobiology!" in *Humanist in Canada* (Spring 1996), 9; 12-14; in a review of *Consilience: The Unity of Knowledge* in the *Journal of Educational Thought*, Vol. 33, No. 2 (August 1999), 191-7; and in "The Humanism of Edward O. Wilson: Toward Consilience" in *Humanist in Canada* (Summer 2000), 26-9; 38.

2 For an explanation of Skinner's essentially humanist position see "The Radical Behaviorism of B. F. Skinner" in Pat Duffy Hutcheon, *Leaving the Cave: Evolutionary Naturalism in Social Scientific Thought* (Waterloo, ON: Wilfrid Laurier University Press, 1996), 399-419.

3 Pat Duffy Hutcheon, "Fear Ignorance, Not Sociobiology!" *Humanist in Canada* (Spring 1996), 9; 12-14.

4 Charles J. Lumsden and Edward O. Wilson, *Promethean Fire: Reflections on the Origins of Mind* (Cambridge, MA: Harvard U. Press, 1983), 23.

5 *Ibid.,* 19.

6 Edward O. Wilson, *Consilience: The Unity of Knowledge* (Toronto, ON: Random House of Canada, 1998), 133.

7 ———————, *Sociobiology: The New Synthesis* (Cambridge, MA: The Belknap Press of Harvard University Press, 1975), 562.

8 For more on this subject, see Albert Somit and Steven A. Peterson, *Darwinism, Dominance and Democracy* (Westport, CT: Praeger, 1997).

9 Thomas Eisner and Edward O. Wilson (Eds.), *Animal Behavior: Readings From Scientific American* (San Francisco, CA: W. H. Freeman and

Co., 1975), 303-315.

10 Edward O. Wilson, *On Human Nature* (Cambridge, MA: Harvard University Press, 1978), 76.

11 ——————, *Naturalist* (Washington, DC: Island Press/Sheerwater Books, 1994), 313.

12 Charles J. Lumsden and Edward O. Wilson, *Promethean Fire: Reflections on the Origins of Mind*, 1983, 31.

13 Edward O. Wilson, *On Human Nature*, 153.

14 ——————, *Sociobiology: The New Synthesis*, 155.

15 ——————, *On Human Nature*, 43.

16 ——————, "The Biological Diversity Crisis: A Challenge to Science" in *Issues in Science and Technology* Vol. 2, No. 1 (Fall 1985), 20-29. See also Wilson's subsequent book, *The Diversity of Life* (New York, NY: W. W. Norton and Co., 1993).

17 ——————, *Consilience: The Unity of Knowledge*, 8.

18 *Ibid.*

19 *Ibid.*, 40.

20 *Ibid.*, 46.

21 *Ibid.*, 902.

22 *Ibid.*, 106. For an enlightening discussion of this issue see Antonio Damasio, *Descartes' Error: Emotion, Reason and the Human Brain* (New York, NY: Putnam, 1994).

23 Edward O. Wilson, *Consilience: The Unity of Knowledge*, 127.

24 *Ibid.*, 130.

25 Robin Fox, *The Search for Society: Quest for a Biosocial Science and Morality* (New Brunswick, NJ: Rutgers University Press, 1989), 112.

26 Edward O. Wilson, *Consilience: The Unity of Knowledge*, 201.

27 *Ibid.* 240.

28 *Ibid.*, 265.

29 *Ibid.*, 7.

17: Richard Dawkins and the Scientific Foundations of Modern Humanism[1]

No one could read The Extended Phenotype, The Blind Watchmaker, The Selfish Gene, Climbing Mount Improbable, River Out of Eden and Unweaving the Rainbow without emerging from that grand, cumulative adventure as a changed person in a considerably altered conceptual world. The objective of this essay is to communicate at least some of the excitement of that experience, as well as the implications for humanism of Dawkins' information and insights—and all this in the space of a few pages. This effort may resemble nothing so much as a 'blind scribbler' setting off to conquer 'Mount Impossible'. Nonetheless, the hope is that, should the arrival elude us, the journey itself may shed a little light.

Richard Dawkins is a British zoologist and ethologist who received his D. Phil. at Oxford, then was briefly on the Faculty at Berkeley before returning to Oxford where he became a Lecturer, then Reader in Zoology, a Fellow of New College, and a contributor to science programming on BBC television. Currently, he is the Charles Simonyi Professor of the Public Understanding of Science at Oxford University. Dawkins appears to have fallen naturally into the role of educator for a public sadly deficient in knowledge and understanding of science. In particular, his writings indicate an early recognition of the need to correct a number of misinterpretations that have crept into popular versions of evolutionary theory.

Identifying the Obstacles

One of the most prevalent modern misconceptions of evolution involves the notion of 'group selectionism'. Dawkins explains that this follows from the mistaken view of the individual (and, by extension, *groups of individuals*) as the fundamental units in the process—rather than the gene. A second common error is known as Social Darwinism. This is a distorted and simplistic belief in wholesale genetic determinism which, when combined with the belief in group selectionism, has too-often provided a pseudo-scientific justification for racism. For over a century this view has been erroneously identified with authentic Darwinism, and communicated to the general public as such by many of its opponents as well as supporters. A third problem involves the idea of 'punctuated equilibrium', introduced and popularized widely by Stephen Jay Gould and Niles Eldridge. This tends to be interpreted by non-scientists (again, erroneously) as a *refutation* of Darwinian evolution.

A fourth widespread misunderstanding of evolution has to do with the notion of transcendental Purpose. This has usually been associated with a commitment to the inevitability of progress, viewed as a generalized improvement in moral as well as material terms and aiming toward some predetermined goal. The fact that evolution is irreversible seems to have contributed to this particular example of 'idealistic nonsense', as Dawkins calls it. But, he points out, irreversibility of process does not imply inevitable progress. On any criterion other than complexity of a specific form and function, evolution can spiral 'downwards' as well as 'upwards.' Although I would think that various ideas popularized by Teilhard de Chardin are most representative of earlier forms of this particular perversion of evolutionary thinking, we now have a new contender. The latest example is the Gaia hypothesis, based on a theory of cosmic evolution which claims that all existence comprises one universal planetary organism. Strangely enough, this highly popularized example of pseudo-science is usually combined with a distorted version of chaos theory, interpreted as implying that reality is random and chaotic, and thus undetermined and indeterminable in its very essence.

Dawkins sees this type of hijacking by pseudo-scientists as only one among a growing number of threats to science in general. He cites another as the populist 'dumbing down' being carried out by some of the so-called science programs on television, and encouraged by certain science educators. There is also the postmodernist bandwagon currently dominating many university departments, which defines science as merely one among a number of equally valid cultural myths. Dawkins notes, as well, that one of the most insidious obstacles to the development of a scientific outlook in the public at large is the ever-increasing torrent of television programs and best-selling books communicating an anti-rational view of the world.

Other sources of confusion and conflict addressed by Dawkins have to do with questions of critical relevance to the social sciences that are not yet adequately answered by evolutionary theory and biology. An example is the issue of whether there is some scientifically warranted sense in which *behavioural patterns* (both mental and physical) develop in a co-evolutionary process along with the evolution of genes. Without asserting a simplistic genetic determinism, can we fruitfully extend the concept of evolution to what appear to be changes over time in incredibly complex phenomena such as human consciousness, customs, ideas and idea systems? All such efforts have been attacked throughout the last century by those who identify a mysterious demarcation in the process: a line creating a special status for the human species. This claim is based on the concept of a 'soul' having been inserted from a non-natural source at some key point in evolution, and is usually justified by an alleged absence in the fossil record of 'the missing link' between humans and other primates. I noticed that a variation of this view even appears in an otherwise excellent book, *Darwin's Ghost*. The author, British geneticist Steve Jones, concludes his compelling clarification and substantiation of Darwinian theory with the following surprising comment: "The Birth of Adam, whether real or metaphorical, marked the *insertion into the animal body* of a post-biological soul that leaves no fossils and needs no genes."[2] [Emphasis added.]

Finally, perhaps the most contentious issue blocking

progress in educating the public about evolution is the question of design. How, it is often asked, could such apparent complexity as the human eye and the reflective mind with its cultural output be possible without an all-knowing Designer? Dawkins' work sheds considerable light on this, and on all the previously mentioned issues as well.

The provision of scientifically warranted responses to these questions is important to humanists for two major reasons. First, we look to such responses for sound and reliable premises about the nature of reality on which to build the ontological foundations of our world view. Second, they have direct relevance for the epistemological and axiological dimensions of modern humanism as well; that is, our assumptions about how human beings can know anything and how we can arrive at credible value judgments. Our answers to these questions, taken together, distinguish scientific or naturalistic humanists from the rest of the population—even from many among the community of professional scientists.

Explaining How Some Genes Survive and Others Don't

The book on this subject, *The Selfish Gene*, is no doubt Dawkins' most notorious production. This is in spite of the fact that it did nothing more than express, in metaphorical language and with meticulous exemplification, the evolutionary theory first introduced by Charles Darwin. The book's objective was to make comprehensible to everyone a theory that has stood the test of time and evidence but, unfortunately, remains widely ignored and stubbornly misinterpreted. For Dawkins, biology is as exciting as any mystery story, and should be presented in all its wonder and with the tools of poetry as well as prose. In approaching Darwinian theory from the 'gene's eye view' he was merely examining the process of natural selection at its roots: from the perspective of the source of variation and the basic unit of heredity. The survival of these heritable entities makes all the difference to the individual organisms or societies or species that (as adaptive vehicles or 'survival machines', or as 'gene communities' composed ultimately of stable systems of genes) either help or hinder transmission into the future. Ever since the idea was popularized by Herbert Spencer, 'survival of the fittest' has been equated with evolution in the public mind. However, Dawkins points out that we can view the process simply as the survival of the fittest genes if, and *only* if, we take 'fittest' to mean the most stable pattern within existing environmental circumstances.

In a subsequent publication, *Unweaving the Rainbow*, Dawkins refers poetically to the genes of a species as "a description of ancestral worlds, a 'Genetic Book of the Dead'."[3] His earlier use of poetic licence to examine this fundamental unit of change in evolution can be seen in the anthropomorphizing ploy of attributing 'selfish' motivations to the gene. However, only the metaphor was original with Dawkins. The critical role of genes (implicit in Darwin's works) had been made explicit as early as 1964 by W. D. Hamilton in his article on "The Genetic Evolution of Social Behaviour"; and in 1966 by G. C. Williams in *Adaptation and Natural Selection*. Nonetheless, the subject seems to have remained little understood beyond a small minority of anthropologists and psychologists—and the new field of sociobiology. Dawkins was only too aware when he began his project in the 1970s that the real implications of Darwinian natural selection had yet to permeate the general public and even most of the scientific community.

Dawkins was careful to emphasize that he was not advocating selfishness, nor a morality based on evolution. "I know," he admitted, "I am in danger of being misunderstood by those people, all too numerous, who cannot distinguish a statement of belief in what *is* the case from an advocacy of what *ought to be* the case... Be warned that if you wish, as I do, to build a society in which individuals cooperate generously and unselfishly towards a common good, you can expect little help from biological nature. Let us try to *teach* generosity and altruism, because we are born selfish."[4]

He explained that, when viewed over the long reaches of geological time and from the standpoint of evolution, individual organisms serve merely as vehicles or colonies for short-lived, unique combinations of genes. Incapable of copying themselves, our bodies are as temporary as dust storms in the desert or a cloud in the summer sky. Each gene, on the other hand, is a discrete particle, existing in the form of a sequence of nucleotyde letters lying between symbols indicating a 'start' and an 'end'. Any such sequence of chromosomal material, if it is to affect evolution, must remain relatively intact as it shuffles and reshuffles down the generations; otherwise it could not function as a replicator of itself. To do this it must have three qualities: longevity, fecundity and copying fidelity. By definition, then, the basic unit of evolution cannot be other than self-serving in terms of the consequences fostered by its presence. This does not, however, translate into an automatic preference for competition over cooperation either in the gene or in the organism in which it is housed. In the positive-feedback process of evolution, development is a matter of *consequences*, not of intentions. Any particular apparatus for survival evolves as a direct result of its success. Genes that happen to operate in conjunction with those particular combinations of other genes to be found in successive bodies are likely, *as a consequence*, to be the survivors over time. This means that, although competition abounds in a nature 'red in tooth and claw', cooperation also plays an important role in evolution. Depending on environmental circumstances, *either* competitive or cooperative processes may contribute to the survival of the genes that practise them, and whose carriers practise them.

Dawkins went on to explain 'Evolutionarily Stable Strategies' and 'kin selection', both of which shed light on how cooperation has functioned throughout evolution. In the first case it appears that, wherever there is a conflict of interest, the responses of social organisms over time result in reconciliations of these that allow most of the participants to win most of the time, and over the long haul. (For example, he quotes the basic ESS rule found in animal species as "if smaller, run away; if larger, attack.") Those who possessed neither the 'hard-wiring' to respond in that way nor sufficient openness to environmental programming in the relevant direction were unlikely to live long enough to reproduce their genes—and hence their propensities for unworkable survival strategies.

Another evolutionarily stable strategy is kin selection. In this phenomenon we find the source of what is known as parental altruism. It seems that the same drive to sacrifice oneself for the survival of one's children operates, to some degree, in other relatives as well. This can be explained evolutionarily by the fact that, in addition to direct offspring, the children of one's siblings carry replicas of one's genes into the future. Thus, the genes of those who happened to value the welfare of their close kin's children tended to win out (in terms of survival) over those genes initiating the opposite behavioural propensities. Perhaps the clearest example of this is the behaviour of members of a bee colony, which is actually one large family. This kind of altruism is limited to close kin, however, and Dawkins notes that attempts to base human social systems on it have failed dismally, due to the preponderance of behaviours stemming from short-sighted competitive self-interest on the part of the majority of citizens. (My own opinion is that, in the absence of a systematically employed socialization process designed to develop social responsibility, misplaced idealism concerning innate human altruism can lead only to the destruction of the commons.)[5]

Dawkins explained how genes do, in fact, exert an influence on the behaviour of their vehicles. It seems they do this indirectly, functioning much in the manner of a computer programmer, albeit one that responds unknowingly to environmental contingencies. "Genes are master programmers," he wrote, "and they are programming for their lives."[6] At some critical point in evolution these 'nature's programmers' became organized into complex organs and ultimately brains, each step in the cumulative development of which resulted in consequences that considerably enhanced their chances of survival. Eventually, the evolution of a capacity to simulate the future gave a gigantic advantage to those fortunate primates who had inherited it. It is a critical aspect of that human form of consciousness which, thus far at least, has made a symbolically based culture and civilization possible for only one species. It has also made possible a form of cultural transmission somewhat analogous to biological evolution.

All this led Dawkins to the conclusion that a new kind of replicator has recently emerged, one that is still in its infancy— its primeval soup. That soup is the soup of human culture, and for the fundamental replicator in this case he suggested the term 'meme'. (He subsequently identified the meme for blind faith as a good example of how such an entity 'selfishly' secures its own survival by discouraging rational and skeptical inquiry.) The general idea that culture evolves in a process isomorphic to that which drives change over time in organic life is a radical and potentially fruitful one. (Jean Piaget was one of the first to propose it, but is seldom credited with the idea.) This model provides us with a conceptual framework for studying the complex interplay between biology and environmental influences in all human behaviour. As Dawkins put it, although it is clear that genes must exert a statistical influence on any behavioural pattern resulting from natural selection, this in no way conflicts with the proposition that such an influence can be modified, overridden or reversed by other influences in the surroundings. "We are built as gene machines and cultured as meme machines," he concluded, "but we have the power to turn against our creators. We, alone on earth, can rebel against the tyranny of the selfish replicators."[7]

If the preceding explanations haven't managed to make all this clear by now, perhaps the following will help sort it out! ....

Avoid the tediousness of faction
Through gene and culture interaction
As scientists you can wax lyrical—
The question has become empirical!

Culture ain't worth a heap of beans
If it can't propagate the genes
But if not fortified by culture
The genes are doomed to quick sepulture.

So let this question lift the gloom
Who gives what or which to whom?
And if you're really very keen
Try empathizing with the gene....

(from "*An Ode to the Selfish Gene*" by Robin Fox)[8]

Defusing the Myth of the Creation of Eternal Souls

The belief expressed in the preceding subtitle is an extremely durable one. It is used to discourage all scientific attempts to explain the two key watersheds in evolution, those marking the origins of life and human consciousness. Dawkins counters the argument for an essentially mysterious, supernatural source of the 'spark of life' and the 'human soul' by pointing out that what lies at the heart of every living thing is something much more knowable. It is information, instructions. The information technology of the genes, he says, is digital, so it appears that the computer may be increasingly fruitful as both metaphor and tool in expanding the public's understanding of evolution. For instance, it helps to view memes as examples of a new form of replicator; as "patterns of information that can thrive only in brains, or the artificially manufactured products of brains—books, computers,..."[9]

This concept promises to shed new light on the implications of evolutionary theory for a science of human behaviour and culture still in its infancy. Dawkins discusses the positive-feedback process characteristic of natural selection and shows how it applies in the case of cultural spirals as well. The concept of 'positive feedback' is used to describe the process by which actions resulting in consequences experienced by the actor as rewarding tend to be repeated—not only by the original initiator but by observers whose capacity for empathy encourages a vicarious sharing of the experience. As a result, the sum of the social rewards flowing from these actions (both real and anticipated) increases exponentially over time. Dawkins cites the example of popular trends and books that become instant best-sellers solely because of the early instigation of just such a cycle of positive reinforcement. Regardless of actual quality, the public perception of worthiness—which the rush of early sales arouses—becomes the spur to further sales. He could also have mentioned the similar behaviour of the stock market.

Because cultural evolution is so many orders of magnitude faster than the biological variety, the concept of positive-feedback spirals raises the question of the likelihood of the former completely taking over the direction and course of the latter. Indeed, recent remarkable breakthroughs in the genome project are providing humankind, at a pace possibly perilous for a population so ignorant of basic science and reliable knowledge about human behaviour, with the means of directing the course of its own biological evolution. Without a grasp of the relationships among scientific knowledge, the technologies made available by it, and the imperative of ethical direction which only wise and humane judgment can provide, human beings may be sadly unprepared for the role now being thrust upon them.

Discovering the Evolutionary Roots of Cooperation

All interactions between surroundings and genes, such as those previously discussed, have their basis in the extended phenotype. This is an important concept with the potential to explain how cooperation functions indirectly in the survival of genes. In the introduction to his book, *The Extended Phenotype*, Dawkins promises a "personal look at the evolution of life and, in particular, the levels in the hierarchy of life at which natural selection can be said to act."[10] He says he is attempting to change the way we have been viewing the gene; to free it from the individual organism in which it has been conceptually imprisoned by theorist and lay person alike. He points out that the gene, as replicator, has extended phenotypical effects. In other words, because it alters the way in which the organism carrying it behaves, a specific gene cannot fail to influence the physical and social environment of that organism—not merely the individual body. And, conversely, any extensive environmental change, because it results in a new set of selective pressures on genes, inevitably affects biological evolution. Dawkins admits to being an interactionist, in the sense of accepting the inevitability of a feedback type of causality operating between biological organisms and their surroundings. (After all, what is the process of natural selection if not one of interaction between environment and organism?) Dawkins emphasizes, however, that the individual gene is itself not altered by this interaction. What is influenced by the web of social relations established by organisms in the form of an extended phenotype is, instead, the probability that any specific gene or combinations of genes will be passed on to the next generation.

As Dawkins explains it, to the extent that *active germ-line replicators* (genes) benefit from the survival of the bodies they inhabit, we will witness adaptations that appear (after-the-fact) to have been for the 'good' of the individual. Similarly, to the extent that the genes gain an indirect benefit from the survival of neighbouring bodies such as other members of the clan, it will appear to observers that adaptation is 'for' the survival of the group. However, in each case, it is the gene as replicator that is the ultimate beneficiary.[11] These insights can also help us understand what natural selection means at the *species level*. Evolutionary adaptation does not operate 'for the good' of the species; nor is the species, as such, a replicator. It is, rather, *the gene pool* of the species that can be said to act in that capacity—but then only when it is reproductively isolated from other gene pools.

Ultimately, success, for either the gene or meme, amounts to vertical transmission down the archives of the species. However, an essential criterion for that success is the particular action, or set of actions, induced by the replicator in its typical or average carriers. We are referring to those specific phenotypic manifestations which happen to have important consequences for survival in a particular time and place. They provide a powerful set of pressures for selection in the context of the immediate social and physical environment. This results in the sideways or environment-specific transmission of genes (and memes): a process which, in turn, interacts with the vertical (down-the-generations) transmission in a co-evolutionary adaptive process. To drive this understanding home, Dawkins uses the example of homosexuality in the human species. "Even if there are genes which, in today's environment, produce a homosexual phenotype," he says, "this does not mean that in another environment, say that of our Pleistocene ancestors, they would have had the same phenotypic effect... Changes in environments may change the very phenotypic characteristics we set out to explain."[12]

The concept of *the extended phenotype* allows us to recognize anew the important role of cooperation in evolution. It helps us understand how mutually compatible sets of genes arise in gene pools at the level of the organism and species, and how complex organs and behaviours evolve within and among organisms. According to Dawkins, "the phenotypic effect of a gene is best seen as an effect on the world at large, and only incidentally upon the individual organism—or any other vehicle—in which it happens to sit."[13] I would like to insert here that, although when we speak of 'the world at large' we usually think of physical surroundings, we should remember that one important aspect of that world is human society, and the culture produced by it. *The extended phenotype* thus opens the door to a clearer understanding of the implications of modern evolutionary theory for the social *as well* as the physical sciences.

Searching For the Origins of Complex Design

In his book, *The Blind Watchmaker,* Dawkins directly tackles the question of design which is at the root of the widespread inability or refusal by the general public to accept the theory of evolution. He puts the issue in perspective by reminding us that "the objects and phenomena that a physics book describes are simpler than a single cell in the body of its author."[14] No wonder so many people assume that there must have been a Creative Designer to have produced this 'miracle' of complex, purposeful life! Nonetheless, Dawkins maintains, "there is nothing supernatural, no 'life force' to rival the fundamental forces of physics"[15]—even when the object to be understood is humankind. There is, instead, a hierarchy of sub-components within sub-components, none of which—no matter how complex the internal relations—disobeys the laws of physics. The task of biologists as evolutionary scientists is to work their way down the hierarchy of life until they reach units so simple that the cause-and-effect relationships involved are relatively easy to ascertain and check.

The biologist's problem, says Dawkins, is the problem of complexity, and it is here that the new chaos theory (appropriately utilized) really comes into its own. He maintains that those who cling to the argument that complexity of result implies a prior plan and a designer to carry it out have been doubly crippled—first, by a failure to grasp fully the immensity of the time involved in evolution; and second, by an intuitive mis-application of probability theory to the process. The latter indicates a confusion of evolutionary change with *randomness*.

Indeed, each of the successive small changes in evolution was simple enough, relative to its immediate predecessor, to have been the result of a random mutation. Nonetheless, the entire sequence of cumulative steps leading to the production of complex organs, etc., was *anything but random*. Natural selection is a *cumulative* process directed after-the-fact by *non-random survival*. This means that, *given* the sum of the critical alterations selected in each of the successive generations leading to a particular phenotype, it is the *consequences* of that individual organism's actions and of the environmental contingencies at the time (including the actions of neighbouring individuals) that determine whether its genes will be carried on in succeeding organisms. There is thus no long-term goal in evolution. But neither is the process entirely random. Dawkins compares cumulative selection to an efficient searching procedure which operates very much like the creative intelligence of an individual working on the basis of trial-and-error.

The ultimate description of this process is provided in a chapter in the book, *Climbing Mount Improbable*, called "The Forty-fold Path to Enlightenment." It deals with the subject of the evolution of the eye. Here Dawkins demonstrates how even the slightest improvement in a capacity to sense movements, or light and shadow, in the surroundings can favour the selection of those organisms possessing the relevant feature. This should finally put to rest the tired old argument that anything as complex as the human eye could not possibly have evolved according to natural selection. The central message of the chapter is that "nothing is as difficult to evolve as humans imagine it to be."[16] It has now been shown by means of computer modelling that it would have required less than half a million years for the lens eye to evolve—a relatively brief span in terms of geological time. In fact, Dawkins points out that eyes have evolved independently at least forty times. These eyes have varied as to the details of their retinas and lenses, whether they were camera-like or compound and, if the latter, whether they featured apposition or various kinds of superposition. Dawkins begins and ends the chapter by quoting Darwin, first with the famous passage in which doubts were voiced about the possibility of the eye being formed by such a simple process as natural selection; and finally, with Darwin's not so well-known conclusion which goes as follows:

> Reason tells me that, if numerous gradations from an imperfect and simple eye to one perfect and complex, each grade being useful to its possessor, can be shown to exist, as is certainly the case; if, further, the eye ever slightly varies, and the variations be inherited, as is likewise certainly the case; and if such variations should ever be useful to any animal under changing conditions of life, then the difficulty of believing that a perfect and complex eye could be formed by natural selection, though insuperable by our imagination, cannot be considered real.[17]

Puncturing Punctuationism

Dawkins has tackled yet another of the sources of confusion about evolution currently dominating public discourse. He thinks great harm was done by the resurrection of the old 'saltation theory' and the consequent boost to Creationism inadvertently brought about by exaggerations and misleading publicity surrounding the work of Stephen Jay Gould and Niles Eldridge. He faults these biologists most for presenting their findings as being radically opposed to neo-Darwinism, rather than as merely the logical implications of Darwinian theory which they actually were. He maintains that, in the fullest and most serious sense, Eldridge and Gould are just as gradualist as Darwin ever was. Their claim to originality rested on a hypothesis which identified the existence of gaps in the fossil record as evidence that most of the change occurring in and among organisms had been compressed into brief bursts. It turns out that they were merely describing certain episodes of relatively rapid evolution initiated by catastrophic alterations of the surrounding environment; and then declaring with great fanfare what should have been the unsurprising conclusion that natural selection does not proceed at a constant rate. But, Darwin never suggested that it did!

According to Dawkins, Gould's *Wonderful Life* "is a beautifully written and deeply muddled book."[18] He considers the theory wrung from the fossils of the Burgess Shale to be a rather sorry mess. The Burgess Shale is the name for a unique set of quarries located high in the Rocky Mountains near the Eastern boundary of British Columbia, Canada. It contains fossilized products of the Cambrian explosion which collectively exhibit a range of disparity in anatomical design considerably exceeding that found in the entire world today. In the book Gould expressed amazement on discovering we humans came 'that close' to not being alive at all; and that the entire process was 'contingent' upon the survival of one particular small set of the profusion of designs then in existence!

However, anyone who understands the contingent nature of all natural selection would wonder, upon reading this particular work of Gould's, what all the fuss was about. Dawkins offers an intriguing explanation for the continuing resistance of evolutionists such as Gould to orthodox Darwinism. He says it is due to a world view fundamentally rooted in pre-Darwinian 'essentialism'. "Gould is hamstrung by dyed-in-the-wool Platonic ideal forms. He really seems unable to comprehend that animals are continuously variable functional machines."[19] I would add that, like all essentialists and dualists, Gould appears, at times, to confuse the taxonomy with the reality it has been employed to organize. I would suggest, as well, that the closet dualism shared by many biologists today cripples them in the battle against the Creationists and 'Intelligent Design' enthusiasts, and is one of the major reasons why the theory of evolution is still under concerted attack in a so-called scientific culture.

Dawkins also discusses the perseverance of Creation myths, noting that many owe their claim to legitimacy to the alleged absence of a known intermediate species between chimpanzee and human. His only comment about these myths is "firstly, they are superfluous, and secondly, they assume the existence of the main thing that we want to explain, namely organized complexity."[20] As for the 'missing link' used by the Creationists as a weapon against the theory of evolution, the idea of a need for this is based on the belief that all life is linked in only one ladder of descent. That idea can be traced to 'the great chain of being' which was an ancient, pre-evolutionary notion. Ironically, says Dawkins, no one who really understands evolution would look for a living intermediary between chimpanzees and humans. Evolution resembles not so much a single chain as a branching tree. Our last common ancestor lived as recently as five million years ago and our two species share approximately 99 percent of all our genes.

Emphasizing the Digital and Hierarchical Nature of Evolution

One of Dawkins' major contributions has been to elaborate in simple terms the implications of Darwin's revolutionary idea about how extreme complexity of design can result from nothing more mysterious than the fact of *non-random* reproduction fuelled by *random* hereditary variation, and accumulating over long reaches of geological time. With the aid of complexity theory and insights from the digital nature of computer programming, he explains, in language comprehensible to the average literate reader, how it is possible to view the evolving product of this process as a hierarchy of systems emerging out of systems, from simple to increasingly complex.

In a delightful little book called *River Out of Eden*, Dawkins discusses the incredible good fortune of those of us who are alive; for, he reminds us, we are the ones whose ancestors had what it takes to survive infancy. He describes each generation as a sieve filtering out the least workable genes in the currents of the river. It is the river of DNA. It flows through time instead of space, and it has been flowing in an unbroken line for at least three thousand million years. It began as one stream—a single ancestor, probably in Africa—and continuously forked over time as, one by one, existing species divided into two. For, after all, it is a digital stream.

Possibly the most illuminating, and potentially revolutionary, of Dawkins' explanations is the one in which he applies complexity theory to show how replicators function in terms of thresholds of development. At certain key transition points one minor alteration in contingent conditions can trigger the formation of new units operating according to new regularities. This has enormous potential for an interdisciplinary evolutionary approach to the study of social science. Dawkins was not the first to deal with this but, as a biologist, his views lend credence to the pioneering insights of Thomas and Julian Huxley and George Herbert Mead, as well as to the more recent work of Edward O. Wilson, physicist Murray Gell-Mann, neuroscientist Roger Sperry and others.[21]

According to Dawkins, the initial threshold in evolution was the appearance of the first replicator—the one event that set the entire process in motion within the river of time. This was a self-copying system in which a rudimentary form of hereditary variation was made possible by occasional random errors in the copying. It marked the beginning of natural selection. Threshold 2 was the emergence of the phenotype, a critical advance marked by the fact that replicators began to survive not by virtue of their own properties, but because of their effects on the vehicle (or phenotype) which they inhabited in conjunction with other genes. Number 3 is the Replicator Team Threshold. Genes tend to prosper when they work in teams. As a key example of this we can think of eukaryotic cells—those bacterial colonies that appeared about 1.4 billion years ago and formed the building blocks of more complex forms of life. Threshold 4, according to Dawkins, was the Many-Cells transition. Many-celled organisms grow differently than do crystals, in which each cell is a miniature version of the whole. The former resemble, rather, the construction of a building from the bricks that make it up.

Number 5, the Nervous-System Threshold, came next. It made possible aggregations of data-handling units such as brains that were capable of making connections between impulses coming in through sense organs and internal recording devices of various kinds. This led to Number 6, the Neuron Threshold, the most important consequence of which was the emergence of animal sentience and the primitive gesturing communication that set the stage for Threshold 7—the onset of symbolic language and human self-consciousness. Number 8 is the Cooperative Technology

Threshold, heralding the emergence of the meme as a new kind of self-replicating entity. Dawkins hypothesizes that humankind may be on the point of experiencing two additional transition points: Number 9, the Radio Threshold and Number 10, that of Space Travel.

Drawing Conclusions

Dawkins notes that science shares with religion the claim to answer fundamental questions concerning the origin and nature of life and the cosmos—with one important difference. That difference is, while scientific beliefs are held tentatively on the basis of evidence, religious ones rely only on faith and the authority of myth. And the problem facing us all is that, if humankind is to survive, myth must at some point give way to fact. Almost unbeknownst to the general public, the digital breakthrough leading to the computer age has revolutionized molecular biology and, consequently, evolutionary theory. Dawkins tells us that the machine code of the genes, operating at the very core of life, can now be recognized as uncannily computer-like. The discovery of the double helix in 1953 had, in fact, already dealt the final blow to every form of Vitalism, with its premise that there is some *essential* difference between living and non-living material. All this would seem to pose an increasingly serious problem for transcendentally based religions, given that these can now clearly be seen as rooted in pre-scientific beliefs. Perhaps this explains the increasingly desperate opposition to evolutionary theory—particularly to its applications in sociobiology—in large segments of the public.

Science also shares with religion the claim to being a source of wonder and awe at the marvels of nature. The difference here is that, with science, the wonder arises from a gradual uncovering of order beneath the apparent confusion. Religious teachings, on the other hand, imply a godlike arbitrariness and unknowable mystery at the very heart of existence. Dawkins' comment on the matter is: "I believe that an orderly universe, one indifferent to human preoccupations, in which everything has an explanation even if we still have a long way to go before we find it, is a more beautiful, more wonderful place than a universe tricked out with capricious, *ad hoc* magic."[22]

Dawkins claims that Darwin made it intellectually legitimate to jettison belief in supernatural forces or gods. I would like to add that Dawkins himself, with his meticulous research and reasoning (not to mention his powerful poetic metaphors) has done much to render that choice *morally and aesthetically imperative* as well. This means that the philosophy of humanism, with its naturalistic and atheistic ontology, its epistemology of agnosticism, and its powerful ethic of human responsibility for the future, is more important than ever before. It only remains for humanists to articulate this perspective clearly and communicate it widely, along with the necessity for the kind of moral wisdom and measured, scientific approach to human affairs that our rapidly expanding knowledge has now made critical to the very survival of our species and other forms of life on earth.

NOTES

1 A shortened version of this article appeared in *Humanist in Canada* (Autumn 2000), 6-11.

2 Steve Jones, *Darwin's Ghost: The Origin of Species Updated* (Toronto, ON: Doubleday Canada, 1999), 330.

3 Richard Dawkins, *Unweaving the Rainbow: Science, Delusion and the Appetite for Wonder* (Boston, MA: Houghton Mifflin Co., 1998), xii.

4 ————————, *The Selfish Gene*, 2nd. Ed. (Oxford, UK: Oxford University Press, 1989), 3.

5 For an elaboration of this idea, see Pat Duffy Hutcheon, *Building Character and Culture* (Westport, CT: Praeger, 1999), 155-76.

6 Richard Dawkins, *The Selfish Gene*, 62.

7 *Ibid.*, 201.

8 This is an excerpt from a poem published in Robin Fox, *The Passionate Mind: Sources of Destruction and Creativity* (New Brunswick, NJ: Transaction Publishers, 2000), 180.

9 Richard Dawkins, *The Blind Watchmaker* (New York, NY: W. W. Norton, 1986), 158.

10 ————————, *The Extended Phenotype* (Oxford, UK: W. H. Freeman and Co., 1982), v.

11 *Ibid.*, 84-5.

12 *Ibid.*, 38.

13 *Ibid.*, 117.

14 Richard Dawkins, *The Blind Watchmaker*, 2.

15 *Ibid.*, 10.

16 Richard Dawkins, *Climbing Mount Improbable* (New York, NY: W. W. Norton, 1996), 196.

17 *Ibid.*, 197.

18 Richard Dawkins, Review of *Wonderful Life* in *The Sunday Telegraph* (February 25, 1990), 1-3.

19 *Ibid.*, 3.

20 Richard Dawkins, *The Blind Watchmaker*, 316.

21 For more on this see Pat Duffy Hutcheon, *Building Character and Culture*, 24-6 and 178-81.

22 Richard Dawkins, *Unweaving the Rainbow*, xi.

18: Changing Perspectives on Free Will: An Example of Cultural Evolution[1]

One of the least-understood aspects of evolutionary naturalism has been what it implies for the classical philosophical issue of free will versus determinism. This becomes even more intriguing when considered in the context of the results of recent scholarship in the behavioural and neuropsychological sciences, and in sociobiology.

Is there such a thing as free will? This is a burning question for many humanists who have come to feel that, although their ethical life stance both implies and demands the possibility of autonomous choice, the conclusions of science cast doubt on that very possibility. The dilemma is not new. The 'free will *versus* determinism' issue has been key to philosophical discourse in every age, if only because the justice systems of all civilized societies have been based inevitably on the proposition that individuals are responsible for their own behaviour. In the end, the position on free will taken by most people in every historical era has come down to their beliefs about the nature of causality: beliefs implied by the world view prevalent at the time. Modern notions about the nature of causality tend to come from one of three sources: (1) the philosophical dualism justifying most of the world's religious belief systems, which defines the human as different in kind from other aspects of nature—and thus not subject to nature's regularities as discoverable by science; (2) the mechanistic determinism underlying the world view presumably warranted by the theory and evidence from physics concerning the nature of reality; and (3) the 'sovereign ego', anti-science type of non-determinism propounded by the Existentialists from Kierkegaard on. For modern scientific humanists this has seemed like Hobson's choice.

The purpose of the present essay is to demonstrate that our confusion and concern are unnecessary. I am suggesting that, although humanists have been right in accepting science as the source and final arbiter of any conclusions on the 'free will *versus* determinism' question, they have been wrong in the choice of physics as the field to which they turned for guidance. The point is that neither Newtonian nor Einsteinian physics—nor the tool of quantum mechanics—is significant for the issue of human freedom. This is because *they do not deal with causal relations at the organic level of existence.* I will argue that there does, in fact, exist a scientific model that allows for a limited concept of human freedom—if not the 'sovereign will' for which some people yearn. It is the emerging evolutionary paradigm now providing a new, interdisciplinary conceptual framework for the organic and the psycho-social sciences: those studies most directly relevant to human beings.

The idea that science might warrant a limited concept of free will is clearly expressed in the writings of David Hume. He departed from most Enlightenment thinkers in his stand on the issue, in choosing to ignore the role of any supersensual order as the source of 'natural law' and to concentrate, instead, on the universality of cause and effect in nature. He thought that, within this all-encompassing process, free will does indeed play a role—in spite of the obvious fact that human behaviour, like everything else in the natural world, is to a large extent predictable. He maintained that all legal and ethical systems are founded on this critical premise, and its denial would seem to contradict common sense. Hume argued that, although each individual act is really the *effect* of the acting person's character and motives (and is thereby, in an indirect sense, determined) the person can always choose *not to act* in any given situation. In his view it is the human process of making inferences on the basis of experience that opens up this possibility. Given the science of the time, however, it is not surprising that the significance of Hume's intriguing idea was then little understood.

The Implications of Darwin's Concept of Feedback Causality in Evolution

It was not until near the end of the nineteenth century that Hume's lead began to be followed up. A new scientific model was now on the scene: an evolutionary model that would seem to imply a distinctive approach to causality for the organic level of relations. However, as Haeckel noted so despairingly, social theorists were slow to accept the idea that they must look for guidance to the process of evolution rather than to an incompatible combination of physics and theology. The prevailing cultural dualism made it difficult to comprehend that Darwinian theory had, for the first time, made the origin and unique role of humans in the ongoing stream of evolution fully explainable in scientific terms.

One of the most important and least understood aspects of Darwinism was what it said about the nature of causality—and, by implication, about the role of the human *will* in the universal causal process. Darwin had discovered that the vehicle of natural selection which emerged with life operates according to positive feedback: a process representing a new kind of cumulative and 'after-the-fact', or contingent, causality. This means that the consequences of the animal's operations on the environment feed back to affect (either positively or negatively) the events to follow, and so on and on. Each response alters the nature of the animal's surroundings and thus, in time, the ways in which those impinging environmental circumstances cause it to behave. The simpler mechanistic form of causality common to the non-organic entities of physics no longer applies under these conditions.

Darwin hypothesized that nothing more mysterious than a gradual accumulation of tiny advantageous changes produced by such contingent operations had produced all of the complex structures of even the highest mammals—including human brains and the so-called spiritual processes of mind, soul and will. His theory implied that the *consequences* of the organism's activities within its environment feed back to become, in turn, the *causes* of subsequent species-change. These consequences include both the impact of the organism on its environment and the degree to which it is successful in producing offspring. This makes the organism's *actions* and resulting environmental effects critical to the entire process of evolutionary change. The resulting emphasis on new definitions of the sources of these actions, for the first time within an evolutionary framework, had at last made possible a social-psychological and neuro-scientific (rather than metaphysical) approach to the age-old question of 'free will *versus* determinism'.

Contributions of the Social Behaviorists

This development would have been earthshaking for philosophy and theology if its significance had been widely recognized. In fact, it was not until near the turn of the century that there occurred the first signs of a satisfactory new resolution of the age-old 'free-will' dilemma: one abundantly compatible with the findings of modern science. It was demonstrated originally in the theorizing of John Dewey and George Herbert Mead and supported by the research of Ivan Pavlov. All three recognized that thinkers such as Herbert Spencer and Sigmund Freud—who had shaped the psychological and social studies of the time—had missed the significance of the critical reversal of causality implicit in natural selection. Unlike those nineteenth century determinists, the 'social behaviorists' began with the premise that the mechanistic causality of physics does not apply at the level of psychological and social interaction. Their approach was based instead on the role of functional circuitry, or contingent feedback, at all levels of the life process—as explained for the first time by John Dewey in his revolutionary 1896 article called "The Reflex Arc Concept in Psychology." Dewey's enlightening new perspective on this concept opened up the possibility of a radical reformulation of the origin and role of conscious *choice* in human affairs, and promised to make the older 'free-will *versus* determinism' argument obsolete.

In spite of working in virtual isolation in Russia, Ivan Pavlov contributed most of the groundbreaking data to support the new perspective. It was the American Pragmatists John Dewey and George Herbert Mead, however, who provided the conceptual framework. Both surmised that the system of human self-consciousness is instigated not by a non-natural spirit or *élan vital* (as the dualists and Vitalists would have it) but by means of goal-seeking behaviour involving the brain's organization of internalized cultural perspectives. They concluded that it is this same operation—when raised to the level of public discourse where a comparison of private perceptions is made possible—that gives rise to *universalized reflection*, or science. Dewey provided an early explanation of how the process of 'willing' (as a key aspect of reflection) could have evolved out of the clash of habits instigated by a problematic situation in the environment: habits which (as learned regularities in experience) had gradually overlaid inherited instincts. Ivan Pavlov's work on conditioned reflexes served to confirm Dewey's theories, as well as to support his own hypotheses concerning the way in which organisms are able to adapt to changing environments through acquired responses built upon those spelled out in the genes.

Pavlov had viewed the common human sensation of 'willing' as the beginning, rather than a satisfactory end point, of inquiry. He hypothesized that the causes of all animal behaviour—including that of humans—were to be found outside, rather than inside, the organism. This led him to the discovery that inherited neural connections or reflexes are not immutable, but subject to change with altered circumstance. He discovered that reflexive responses can be elicited not just by stimulation of the relevant organs, but by *new cues in the environment*—providing these have been consistently associated with the original occurrence of the response. The broader implications of this were driven home for Pavlov when it became clear that, with the breakthrough into language, the human primate had evolved a sophisticated 'second signalling system'. This system allowed for a virtually unlimited source of stimulation for increasingly complex behaviours such as remembering, imagining and the weighing of alternative possibilities. The older assumptions of a dualism of mind and brain were no longer necessary. Nor was the accompanying belief in a sovereign ideal realm capable of determining the material one—or *vice versa*.

The work of the Pragmatists complemented that of Pavlov to a remarkable degree. It is unfortunate that this agreement was obscured by the use of differing terminology, and by the subsequent absence within the academic community of inter-disciplinary communication among scholars committed to competing models. Dewey referred to habits and instincts, rather than to conditioned and unconditioned reflexes, but he arrived at the same place by the philosophical route of Pragmatism that the Russian researcher had attained by precise experiment. Not surprisingly, their work also led the two men to similar conclusions concerning the possibility and limits of free will. Dewey claimed that the habits built upon instinctive behaviour are the sole agents of our mature abilities of recollection, foresight and judgment, and "a mind or soul in general which performs these operations is a myth."[2]

The Method of Intelligence

Dewey's conclusion was that only by understanding the process of valuing can we achieve a modern understanding of free will. The only element of freedom open to humans, he said, resides in that intimate relationship between knowing and valuing at the very core of the 'method of intelligence' which the Pragmatists referred to as reflection. They agreed that this element of freedom stems from the possibility of *choice*. The necessity for choice, they said, arises when there is an excess of preferences. If that were not the case the flow of habit would not have been interrupted. When we act out of the sensation of free will that emerges from this clash of preferences we make a choice. Choices can be dictated by custom or momentary impulse; or they can be knowledgeable and reasonable. Whenever choice results from deliberation, the mechanical flow of cause and effect is checked while the chooser visualizes a number of possibilities and predicts the consequences most likely to flow from each. At some point "the moment arrives when the imagination pictures an objective consequence... which supplies an adequate stimulus, and releases definitive action."[3]

According to Dewey, deliberative choice involves valuing. Valuing is the *act of judging* which of all possible future experiences are likely to be the most desirable over the long term. He described it as "the constructing of enjoyable objects [ends] directed by knowledge of consequences... a change from looking to the past to looking to the future."[4] It was clear to Dewey that reasoning and valuing are integral aspects of the method of intelligence and not at all in opposition—as both the traditional philosophies and the proponents of the then-new Phenomenology and Existentialism would have it. He suggested that, while humans can choose without making value judgments, *reasonable* choice is impossible without valuing, just as valuing is impossible if the method of intelligence is not employed. Dewey always maintained that, in the absence of reasoned thought, we can only *feel* various shades of enjoyment as they occur haphazardly in current circumstances. We cannot control their presence in the experience to come. Thus, he said, do we lose our freedom to shape the future!

Dewey recognized three requirements for whatever degree of free will is possible within the human continuum of experience and nature. These are: (1) the efficiency to execute actions, (2) the capacity to change plans, and (3) the power of desire and choice to affect events. He explained the first by noting that only reliable knowledge of the connections among experienced events can give us the efficiency to execute actions in the pursuit of goals. Regarding the second requirement, he said that the capacity to change plans depends upon the ability to imagine alternative paths and their predictable consequences. And, finally, he reminded us that only by valuing certain consequences over others do we allow desire and choice to affect the course of future experience. Without the habits of thought and action arising from these abilities we are indeed helpless pawns in an externally determined universe: prisoners of rigid custom on the one hand, and of unrestrained impulse wherever custom does not dictate the rules.[5]

Pavlov would have agreed. He once remarked that freedom of choice for human beings is realizable only in proportion to our tested knowledge about how the processes determining our action actually work. In this way only, he claimed, through scientific understanding of human functioning, can we hope to attain the control over human nature that we have achieved over that which is external to us. Pavlov saw such control simply as the power of knowledgeable human choice to affect consequences. Some years later, B. F. Skinner referred to freedom in the same terms and was often misunderstood because of this. Skinner's model of operant conditioning extended the Pavlovian revolution by defining the precise reinforcing role of consequences in even the most complex aspects of human learning. His findings also supported the conclusion of the Pragmatists that what has traditionally been viewed as free will is neither "a mystical cause of action or an inaccessible ritual, but a function of action itself, subject to analysis within the concepts and techniques of the natural sciences and ultimately to be accounted for in terms of controlling variables."[6]

Significance of the Concept of Hierarchy in Evolution

Julian Huxley was an evolutionary theorist and younger contemporary of Dewey and Mead who addressed the issue of free will in the early part of the century. He employed Mead's concepts of 'emergence' and 'contingency' to explain evolution as a hierarchy of systems of feedback relations in nature, each emerging as an increasingly complex state from an earlier simpler one. In each case the emergence was precipitated by some change occurring in environmental conditions obtaining at the previous level of relations. It required no injection of cosmic Spirit or *élan vital* at any stage in the process. Consequently, "fate [for humans] is the limiting force of heredity and environment; and freedom is human plasticity—the variety of possible development opening before a man endowed with a definite heredity."[7] Huxley concluded that Darwinian evolutionary theory implies a world and future where humanity is *both* determined and free.

In the 1960s the Nobel Prizewinner Roger Sperry incorporated these earlier insights into a model of neurological functioning based on the evidence from his own groundbreaking research on the two hemispheres of the brain. He went a step beyond his intellectual forebears, however, attempting to show that, at each evolutionary breakthrough, the higher-level system is able to function in a causal capacity over the previous levels.[8] An intriguing implication of this is that the principle can be applied to the systems of organic life, consciousness and culture. Cultural beliefs tend to shape social rituals and the resulting behaviours of individuals—just as the latter produce changes at the level of psychological functioning which, in turn, can build upon or inhibit the neurological responses programmed in the genes. This would seem to confirm the work of Pavlov and Skinner on the role of conditioning and reinforcement. It also justifies the claims of theorists such as the turn-of-the-century French sociologist Emile Durkheim who said that we are not warranted in 'reducing' social behaviour to psychological facts, or psychological facts to the units of analysis employed in biology—even though what is discovered about the constitution of each level is a significant and not-to-be-ignored aspect of the more encompassing emergent one. Modern cognitive neuroscience proceeds according to the same premise.

Sperry's theory is also supported by recent evidence from psychological neuroscience demonstrating a connection between what committed believers describe as a mystical experience initiated by religious disciplines (such as fasting and meditation) and the sensation of self-transcendence accompanying the mob hysteria associated with various group rituals involving consistent rhythmic chants or drumbeats. Researchers have also found that the same condition can be induced by suggestion—in the case of people previously conditioned by prevailing cultural mythologies to expect such an experience. (Note the 'Jerusalem Syndrome' which is manifested in Christian pilgrims in terms of a belief that 'the second coming' of Jesus is imminent, while their Jewish counterparts are invariably obsessed with pending visitations of the Messiah!)

Researchers have also discovered that this 'mystical' sensation can be produced mechanically by probing designated areas of the brain, as well as chemically by means of hallucinogenic drugs.[9] This is a compelling example of how contingent or feedback causality can operate from various emergent levels of interaction (the chemical, neurological, psychological, social and cultural) to bring about what is interpreted by the 'experiencer' as identical (and equally mysterious and uncaused) feeling states. In many cases the initiating behaviour tends to become compulsive and addictive; in other words, it is increasingly less open to the power of reasoned choice. This should not be surprising in view of the fact that the person involved is convinced that an ultimately desirable, mystical consummation has been effected by some extrasensory contact between the individual's 'sovereign will' and the Absolute: a contact that presumably can occur only when cognitive activity has been suspended.

Conclusions

Like the earlier work of Pavlov, these modern research findings lend compelling support to the theory spelled out first by the early Pragmatists. What, then, does all this mean for the concept of free will? Is it possible to begin to spell out the shape of an emerging paradigm—rooted in current scientifically confirmed premises concerning causality—that would be acceptable to scientific humanists? I am convinced that a focus on the role of contingency in human actions points the way to a satisfying resolution of the dilemma. Psychological neuroscience would seem to provide confirmation that the human is indeed an open system in a hierarchy of open systems constituting the ongoing stream of evolution. We *do* respond to contingencies which, in turn, have resulted partly from our own thrusts into the totality of our physical and social world. Social scientists tell us that among the most powerful of these causal factors are social rituals and the myths that have informed and driven our group-created cultures from ancient times. In the words of social behaviorists, only to the degree that we possess reliable knowledge about the causes and consequences of our actions can we achieve freedom to alter our previously conditioned behaviour—or what we impulsively choose to do. This knowledge encourages us to reflect on the consequences of previous actions and to 'will' to act in ways that will engender desired future consequences. Cultural beliefs that explain behaviour and feelings in terms of unknowable forces and beings are thus, by definition, the enemies of whatever degree of free will is available to humans.

There is now considerable evidence to indicate that, from the moment of birth, each human being begins to forge a character from what genetic potential makes of experience. We also have good reason to conclude that the value system defining that character determines the nature of our choosing.[10] Given the content of my values and knowledge at the moment of choice—and the precipitating circumstances—it is true that I could have done no other than what I did. This does not translate into 'sovereignty' of will, but it does mean that my choice is *unique to me*. For modern scientific thinkers, free will is meaningful only in terms of this capacity for choice—and reflective choice at that. No freedom, however limited, can exist if behaviour remains merely habitual or impulsive—or if it is driven by demonic notions that our ancestors embedded in the culture. We now know that, as living, culture-creating organisms, we form an inextricable part of nature's continuous current of cause-and-effect. None of the findings of modern science indicate a possibility of altering or re-directing the process from the outside. It seems clear that we can only work from within. The obvious conclusion from all this is that free will, in the sense of the old notion of a sovereign ego operating *upon* a material reality, is merely the stuff of dreams and wishes. But this does not imply determinism as it was formerly understood. Precisely *because* of humanity's involvement in nature's current of cultural evolution, we *necessarily* affect its direction and velocity.

As John Dewey explained so presciently, a scientifically supportable concept of 'free' will can be viewed as the potential to redirect the course of nature's continuum of cause-and-effect by achieving conscious control of the consequences of our own actions. It means that we can produce different effects than would otherwise have occurred. Our power both to predict and alter effects has been increased exponentially by the progress of science. The positive message in what modern science implies for free will is that we are not condemned to use that power destructively. To the degree that choices are based on reliable knowledge and reason—combined with the ability to imagine and evaluate possible future consequences—we can participate wisely in the uniquely human task of guiding the course of both biological and cultural evolution. As cultural beings we have evolved the potential for reasoned choice, and have been both burdened and privileged with the responsibility that such choice endows. This is what free will represents for humankind at the dawning of the new millennium.

Free Will

"I am a part of all that I have met,
And all that I have met is part of me."
Now sages tell us that the poet's song has meaning sounder yet
Than even he
Could see.
For acts that habit only seems to choose
Exert a claim the will cannot refuse;
And I in time become
The means I use—
The self that governs me.

But still, that self is partly fused within the fire of choice;
I learn to value and to strive for what I yet can be.
My values have their source in all that I have done and known,
They are the fruits of all the seeds
That I have ever sown,
And they, in turn, determine
All the dreams I call my own.
Yet, in the reasoned choice of means
To reach the goals that beckon me—
Within the limits set by nature
And contingency—
I feel my will is free!

NOTES

1 Previously published under the title of "John Dewey and the Problem of Free Will" in *Humanist in Canada* (Spring 1999), 6-10; 13.
2 John Dewey, *Human Nature and Conduct* (New York, NY: Henry Holt, 1922), 176.
3 *Ibid.*, 193.
4 John Dewey, *Individualism Old and New* (New York, NY: Capricorn Books, 1929), 272.

5 Pat Duffy Hutcheon, *Leaving the Cave: Evolutionary Naturalism in Social Scientific Thought* (Waterloo, ON: Wilfrid Laurier University Press, 1996), 202.

6 B. F. Skinner, *Verbal Behavior* (New York, NY: Appleton-Century-Crofts, 1957), 449.

7 Julian Huxley, *Religion Without Revelation* (New York: Harper and Brothers, 1957/1925), 193.

8 Erika Erdmann and David Stover, *Beyond a World Divided* (Boston, MA: Shimbhala, 1991), 149.

9 Barry Beyerstein, "The Brain and Consciousness: Implications for PSI Phenomena", *The Skeptical Inquirer* (Vol. 12, 1987), 162- 73; also, by the same author, "Neuropathology and the Legacy of Spiritual Possession", *op. cit.*(1988), 148-62.

10 Pat Duffy Hutcheon, "Value Theory: Toward Conceptual Clarification," *The British Journal of Sociology* (Vol. 23, No. 2, 1972), 172-187.

Conclusions:
A World View for the
Global Village

The journey we have taken in the previous pages can shed light on many of the concerns and questions puzzling humanists and would-be humanists today. Most important is the fact that, in gazing backward down the 'road to reason' at the origins and evolving nature of this remarkable philosophy—and forward to potential futures through the eyes of those at the forefront of current thought—we cannot help but emerge as different people. Our odyssey makes us appreciate anew the nobility of all those intellectual giants, past and present, who had the wisdom and the courage to shine their torches upon the road ahead. It makes us appreciate, as well, our personal good fortune in having encountered the enduring products of these great minds, and in having acquired the skeptical mind-set and intellectual freedom to examine and assess their insights, and the courage to 'bet our lives' on them.

It is my hope that the journey has helped people drawn to the humanist perspective to identify, in clear and positive terms, the conceptual boundaries of the philosophy which is often referred to so ambiguously. If this book contributes to a sounder understanding of humanism on the part of its current adherents, as well as for those who are dissatisfied with transcendental world views and on the lookout for something better, it will have achieved its objective. The major initial step on the road to that understanding will be the recognition of the one great idea shared by all the founders of what we now call modern humanism.

What is that one great idea and what the source of its power to survive? Our journey points to the conclusion that it is nothing less than a defining premise about existence, and the place of humankind within it. This premise concerns a commonality and continuity among all existing inorganic and organic forms. It asserts that humans are part of the process of the universe, no less natural than any other part. It requires no presumed injection of an unknowable 'spirit' component at any point in the process of our emergence; it offers no mysterious access to a consciousness beyond that created by our joint, cumulative experience of nature. It implies, instead, that human actions and relationships are as subject to causation as are those of any other existing entities. *It is the philosophical premise of evolutionary naturalism.*

This premise has been called by different names at different stages of history: 'monism' in place of all the various versions of the established mind/body and heaven/hell dualism; 'materialism' as distinct from belief in transcendental Spirit or Consciousness; 'atheism' as compared to 'theism'; and 'naturalism' as opposed to 'supernaturalism'. And ever since Darwin, the significance of the evolutionary process as the agent of change within and throughout nature has been recognized as central. However, the basic concept of the human species as an integral aspect of nature has remained the same throughout, and always it has challenged the conventional wisdom of the age.

Perhaps the greatest source of confusion concerning the philosophy of humanism today is the old 'theism *versus* atheism' issue. By a strange solecism, atheism (meaning simply 'non-theism') is often pictured as a doctrinaire stance merely because it implies an absence of belief in the supernatural beings that have, for so long, peopled the conceptual worlds of the majority in every culture. But it defies all the rules of logic to assume the existence of something for which, because of its very nature, no evidence could ever be found while, at the same time, demanding concrete evidence of the posited entity's *non-existence* from those who merely refuse to buy into the assumption. Contrary to what this type of argument would claim, humanists who accept the position of atheism are guilty of neither dogmatism nor nihilism. They *do* believe—albeit tentatively—in an ultimate ontological premise: that of naturalism rather than supernaturalism.

Atheism or 'free thought' is, however, not in itself sufficient as the foundation of any philosophical stance. It is simply the essential first step toward achievement of a comprehensive humanist world view. It can be compared to an unshackling of the legs— making it possible to stride out freely. The road then taken is determined not by that unshackling process; not simply by a *negation* of belief. We have had ample opportunity to learn from the dead end of Existentialism that mere negation of religious belief— burdened as it often is with an unacknowledged and hazardous undertow of moral relativism and/or long-discredited Marxist doctrine—can lead to places where no humanist would want to go. The less-travelled road of modern humanism, on the other hand, is neither set in stone nor impulse-driven and directionless. It is marked by signposts concerning three vital areas of existence. These involve ultimate premises on the basis of which all human beings operate every day of their lives, whether knowingly or otherwise. They comprise beliefs about: (1) the nature of reality (*ontological* premises); (2) the nature of 'the good' (*axiological* premises); and (3) the nature of knowledge (*epistemological* premises). It is the position spelled out on these three components of any world view that distinguishes the 'road to reason' from all those crowded thoroughfares along which 'imaginary friends' have for countless ages chastised and beckoned humankind.

Modern humanists, in choosing the road less travelled, are consciously launching their journey on the premise of evolutionary naturalism. But they go further. They acknowledge that, although an absolutely *necessary* aspect of their world view, this belief is not in itself *sufficient*. They realize that the crucial recognition of human continuity within nature has allowed their intellectual forebears to focus on a second defining premise. It has to do with the *distinctiveness* of our species as the only animal thus far to have developed critical consciousness and culture. This is the source and justification of humanism's emphasis on the significance of the human being in the scheme of things—first, in its role as *knower*, and second, as *artist* and *valuer*.

Modern humanists note that our species is distinctive, as well, in the imaginative capacity that it has evolved for constructing emotionally satisfying *explanations* of what is experienced. Early humans lived in surroundings where little was understood and anything conceivable seemed possible; where few of the events impinging on the group were controllable and most would have been viewed as arbitrary and terrifying. An understandable emotional need for security, coupled with the evolved openness to learning that was rapidly distinguishing them from neighbouring animal species, would have made our ancestors uniquely vulnerable to Animism and magic. It is easy to understand the origins of the habit of attributing events to magical and supernatural 'father figures' whose presumed power to provide protection and a dependable food source for the tribe was circumscribed only by the limits of the evolving imaginations of the shamans and soothsayers.

In time, however, a few members of the tribe must have come to the realization that some ways of explaining experience actually worked to allow them a modicum of control over their surroundings, while others did not. This would have gradually initiated the search for the most *reliable* of possible alternative explanations which, in its turn, led to the first crude beginnings of the scientific process. From that time on there would have been a few enterprising individuals in every generation who suspected that there was, in fact, no need to resort to myths of revelation from on high; or to fictions about mysterious intuitive messages from unknowable forces beyond what is accessible to human experience. And so we come down through the eons to discerning, skeptical thinkers such as the Buddha, and to the birth of formal science in both the Eastern and the Western worlds.

Humanists of the current era, having learned from the pioneering 'road builders' of previous ages, understand the natural origin and use of our evolved instruments for observing and explaining experience and for testing those explanations: our tools of reason, language and the senses. They recognize that only by these means has our species built knowledge with the power to predict, and thus to influence, the course of events. Modern humanists are all-too-aware that other so-called sources of truth have led invariably to costly detours and dead ends for, unlike science, they contain no self-correcting mechanism.

All this helps to explain why humanists today are committed to science as the best method yet discovered for constructing knowledge and testing its reliability. It is why they emphasize the unity or universality of the scientific approach as a means of identifying the operation of cause and effect, in human behaviour and society as well as at the organic and inorganic levels of existence. It is why their epistemology can best be described as one of agnosticism, as Thomas Huxley explained it.

Modern humanists understand that science, broadly and appropriately defined, is merely the disciplined use of the sum of human conceptual abilities in: (1) observing and comparing evidence of 'what actually happened' in historical or experimental situations; and (2) constructing hypotheses and attempting to test or falsify them according to a previously agreed-upon public process of collecting and communicating evidence. The first type of knowledge (which we can call 'historical') describes past or present circumstances as accurately or objectively as possible. It is a necessary component of the second type, our 'scientific' knowledge which provides us with the means to exert a degree of control over the future.

Those propositions which survive the scientific process of inquiry have been shown throughout history to be the most reliable grounds we fallible humans could possibly discover for action. They stem from an approach to knowing that emerged out of that very symbol-manipulating capacity which resulted in our current uniqueness as a species. A primitive version of this same process led our ancestors to the use and control of fire, and to agriculture and animal husbandry. The scientific approach, then, is not merely a matter of taste for humanists, to be applied or ignored at will. It is, instead, essential to the world view of modern humanism, for it is necessarily implied by our *ontological* premises of evolutionary naturalism and human distinctiveness, and by our *epistemological* premise of agnosticism.

It is true that, periodically, the foundations of the humanist world view have been attacked from within by the temporary appeal of Romanticism and subjectivism. Still, there always remained a core of steadfast carriers of the basic message: that what defines and makes possible our precious heritage of humanism is the *method* of open-ended and self-regulated inquiry. These were the people who realized that the authenticity and very survival of a plant depends upon the integrity of its root system.

Such internal attacks were led in the past by well-meaning, self-declared humanists such as Henri Bergson and Jean-Paul Sartre: many of whom began as philosophical naturalists but departed from the approach of science. Typically, they were seduced by the need for certainty, coupled with the siren call of an autonomous 'intuitive' or 'vital' entity within what they needed to believe was the essentially mysterious spiritualistic heart of humankind. Today the same subversive mission is being attempted by various postmodern, Pagan and 'New Age' thinkers, many of whom claim a home in humanism on social/political grounds, or because they have turned away from traditional religion. Their beliefs about the nature, sources and justification of knowledge are very different from those at the roots of humanism, however, and that difference is crucial.

Humanists identify a second aspect of human distinctiveness as our *creative capacity*. They believe the human species has evolved an imagination allowing us to envision possibilities not immediately available in past or current experience. They identify this imagination as the origin of all the gods that have been created in our image throughout history and pre-history. And they value it as the source of our architecture, music, literature and the visual arts. As humanists, they cherish all the magnificent creations of humankind that have enriched world culture throughout the centuries. They cherish them—not because they are inspired by some transcending 'spirit'—but as the products of our remarkable human imagination and technical and communicative skills. Humanists feel that if these products are worthy of reverence, it is *because* of their human origins and inevitable limitations—not in spite of them.

Modern humanism focuses particularly on the significance of a third aspect of human distinctiveness—our *capacity for moral-*

ity. This involves the propensity to acquire personal values and to create cultural ideals that mirror and symbolize and, in turn, transmit these. Morality is assumed to comprise, as well, the capacity to make choices: choices which then function to direct and shape individual characters and thus, ultimately, to provide direction to the very culture that gave them birth. Although this concern for ethics and morality is shared by every theological and philosophical system of thought, humanists differ from all the others in their premises as to the source and justification of—and criteria for—personal values, ethical principles and ideals, and rules for behaviour. They believe that these are grounded in the totality of the experience of the human race, from time immemorial. They recognize no other source. This conjecture provides the *axiological* premise of humanism.

This does not mean that modern humanists are moral relativists. It means that, rather than believing in immutable virtues installed permanently in some supernatural—or even natural—realm, they seek to identify and establish values that are necessary and workable and *universally applicable*. Humanists justify both the need and possibility for these in terms of: (1) the shared evolutionary history and biological drives of our species, some of which require controlling and/or inhibiting while others need to be encouraged by the promotion of appropriate moral guidelines; (2) our shared necessity to function as members of social groups, and thus to develop attitudes, rules and customs conducive to group survival; and (3) our joint responsibility for the future of all life on earth, with the imperative for governing ethical principles that this implies. The ultimate check on such values is assumed to be the test of experience—over the longest possible term and the widest possible expanse of space that might conceivably be touched by the ripples of consequences from our actions. The ultimate criterion for morality in general is viewed as the degree to which the choice based on a particular value judgment is likely to contribute to the long-term welfare of the planet, and to personal fulfilment (or the quality of life over time) for individuals *and* the social groups of which they form an integral part. This criterion implies a central role for justice, kindness, honesty, courage, social responsibility, mutual respect, freedom of belief, peacefulness and democracy in human affairs.

Modern humanists see no *inherent* conflict between the welfare of other forms of life on the planet and that of humankind; or between the social group and the individual. Nothing that imposes cumulative damage on the ecology can benefit the human species in the long term. Nor can anything destructive of the human gene pool be good for the individual organisms condemned to carry and be shaped by those genes. In exactly the same way, nothing that degrades or corrupts human culture in the course of history can be of benefit to the individual, for individual selves are created out of social intercourse, just as organisms are created from the sexual. This is why individual freedom of action—although desirable within limits—can never be the ultimate, absolute, or even a major criterion against which to assess morality. There is widespread agreement among humanists that no one can be granted the right to imperil the evolution of our species, either by overpopulating the globe and/or damaging the physical environment (including other forms of life) which ultimately determines the nature of our gene pool, or by polluting the culture that creates and nurtures our social being.

All this leads to the conclusion that an integrative humanist world view is in the best interests of the emerging global village that will be home to all of humankind in the near future. The ancient myths continuing to nurture inter-group hostilities among our ethnic and national collectivities were created in the context of a vastly different set of environmental circumstances from those facing us today. They evolved among the warring tribes of our collective human past as a response to the need for internal cohesion, and were fed by an often well-warranted distrust, hatred and fear of outsiders. But technology has thrust our species into a planetary proximity and interdependence for which these archaic religious traditions have left us dangerously unfit and unprepared. A new morality and a new philosophy to justify it is imperative.

It is precisely *because* of this recognition of the critical role of morality in the cultural evolution now inevitably shaping even organic evolution, that the subject is central to the world view of humanism. Believing as humanists do that the future course of all evolution (and thus of all life on earth) is determined by the actions of human beings rather than of gods, they are *impelled* to focus on the need for worthy values and ethical principles, and for responsible moral choice. They feel that, as humans, we—*all* of us—can do no other.

In the past, humanist organizations have sometimes made a serious mistake in attempting to define the movement by what they *opposed* rather than what they stood *for*. Merely being against superstition and transcendental religion is, in itself, no guarantee of humanism. Another common error has been to define humanism in political rather than philosophical terms. But the problems faced by humanity are far too complex for us to suppose that any particular program (whether socialist, populist, liberal or conservative) is the only right way to proceed. A commitment to the scientific approach in the search for morally justifiable solutions to society's ills should be seen as an invitation to all who have the intellectual openness to join us in that quest. It implies, as well, a willingness to assess and alter political means continuously, in the light of new evidence gained from experience. Such an approach carries with it no guarantee of 'political correctness' or of timeless truth.

The most important lesson to be learned from the great thinkers whose ideas have shed light upon the 'road to reason' is that humanism can be understood only in terms of the premise of *evolutionary naturalism* as its necessary condition (in contrast to spiritualism, transcendentalism and any other form of dualism). We can conclude from their teachings that it involves as well, three additional beliefs implied by its major defining premise of humankind's common origin with other animals. All three stem from the *distinctiveness* of the human species within that common nature. They have to do with: (1) an emphasis on the process of human knowing, and on the priority and universality of the scientific, empirical approach as a means of building knowledge; (2) an appreciation of the products of human imagination and technical skill; and (3) an overriding focus on morality (with universally applicable humanitarian principles in the role of guideposts) as the unique responsibility of humankind. This, then, is the world view of humanism: a modern world view that might, just possibly, save the emerging global village from self-destruction in the perilous centuries ahead.

Epilogue

Amazing Life

Amazing life, how great the code
that carves a course through me,
to futures yet uncharted from
some long forgotten sea.

No master hand defined my fate.
No gods created me.
Star dust and ocean current sparked
the genes that led to me.

O'er eons of uncounted time,
like shifting dunes of sand;
from grasping paw on groping limb,
evolved the human hand.

Amazing hand, how great the tools
that humankind could wield.
How wide the world that hitherto
from animals was sealed.

But symbols were the crucial key
that opened culture's gate;
for language carried consciousness,
and knowledge in its wake.

Amazing power of human thought
that carves a course through me;
to futures yet uncharted from
some long forgotten sea.

About the Author

Pat Duffy Hutcheon is a sociologist and retired Education professor. A longtime interdisciplinary scholar, her undergraduate degree from the University of Alberta was in education with a major in history; her M.A. from the University of Calgary was in sociology and anthropology; her Ph.D. from the University of Queensland, Australia focused on the social-psychological aspects of sociology; and, during a stint at Yale University on a Fellowship, she had the opportunity to delve into Southeast Asian Studies and social theory. A lifelong interest in the connections between biology and animal/human social behaviour stems from experience as a child and young wife on Canadian prairie farms. She was a secondary-school history teacher before joining the faculty of the University of Regina, where she taught instructional 'methods' in social studies and the sociology of education, eventually becoming Head of the Department of Educational Foundations. Following a period at the University of British Columbia teaching courses in the sociology of education and early childhood education, she served as a director of the Vanier Institute of the Family and as a research advisor to the Health Promotion Branch of the Canadian federal government. She is the author of *A Sociology of Canadian Education* (Toronto, ON: Nelson of Canada, 1975), the first textbook ever published on that subject. Among her many recent publications are *Leaving the Cave: Evolutionary Naturalism in Social Scientific Thought* (Waterloo, ON: Wilfrid Laurier University Press, 1996) and *Building Character and Culture* (Westport, CT: Praeger, 1999). In 2000, she was named 'Canadian Humanist of the Year' by the Humanist Association of Canada, and in 2001, 'Humanist Distinguished Service Awardee' by the American Humanist Association. One can visit Dr. Hutcheon's website at < http://humanists.net/pdhutcheon >.

Index

....